Praise for *Badass Abroad*

"With a strong dose of wit and endearing pragmatism, Claire Hauxwell chronicles the ups and downs of her life as an expat Accompanying Supporting Spouse (or ASS, as she calls it). She shares her engaging journey of personal transformation through courage, authenticity, and self-love. If you're an expat partner looking for insights, tools, and inspiration to embark on your own badass adventure, *Badass Abroad* is the book for you."

Katia Vlachos, PhD, CPCC
Certified Coach & author of *A Great Move: Surviving and Thriving in Your Expat Assignment*

"*Badass Abroad* is a very real portrayal of expat life: global friendships, the good and the bad kind, the resentment and loneliness that creep up on you, losing your way, finding your way, and navigating uncertainty. Claire caps off each chapter with her insights and wisdom. The headings, chapters and hashtags are #delightful."

Rhoda Bangerter
Certified Coach for Accompanying Partners & author of *Holding the Fort Abroad*

"This is the book I'd recommend to every expat accompanying spouse moving abroad today – pack this in your hand luggage! Strong, sassy, witty, honest, sarcastic, sweary, and full of nuggets of wisdom, Hauxwell guides you step by step on how to bloom into a badass abroad."

Mariam Navaid Ottimofiore
Author of *This Messy Mobile Life*

"Claire's story is so relatable that I had to put the book down a few times to metaphorically go and hug my past self. That's even despite the fact that my serial expat journey was wildly different. Whether you moved abroad at your own initiative or you're an accompanying spouse, this is a raw and honest personal story about how life abroad forces you to find yourself and your inner sense of calm, come what may. A must-read!"

Katherine
Bad Days Abroad

"*Badass Abroad* will make you do three things. First, you'll laugh so hard you'll spill your coffee. Then, you'll realize that reading it actually made you smarter. And when you're done, you'll be left with a happy grin on your face. Part memoir, part self-help book, *Badass Abroad* is an entertaining read that's full of surprising twists, relatable stories, and smart advice. A must-read for every expat spouse."

Olga Mecking
Author of *Niksen: Embracing the Dutch Art of Doing Nothing*

"This book has it all for an inspiring, thought-provoking experience with some laugh-out-loud moments. The author crafts an engaging group of stories through her multiple moves as an expat, and she shares what she learned along her journey. She demonstrates how personal growth stems from vulnerability. The book takes an honest look at the human experience through the eyes of change and adaptation. Through her coaching, she offers the readers many opportunities to ignite self-discovery."

Patricia Friberg, MPS ACC NBC-HWC
Personal & Executive Coach, Host of *Learned It From an 80's Song* podcast

"I have often asked myself why it is so hard for us women to just come to the table as we are – perfectly imperfect. In *Badass Abroad* Claire Hauxwell lets us peak into the overseas life of her alter ego, Dandelion. She doesn't shy away from being both vulnerable AND incredibly strong. We follow this heroine's journey on her search of fulfillment while she tries not to get lost in between worlds. There are essential and empowering messages for every badASS out there – those who are done with trailing and would rather take up her blazing trail. The world definitely needs more of this."

Christina Kapaun
Lecturer, sparring partner and coach for global nomads, expats and repats, Intercultural Trainer, stories to be told @southboundstories | s.cope - team for intercultural competence

"I had the privilege of reading this book in advance on an airplane and was getting side-eyes from passengers because it made me laugh out loud. It will also bring tears to your eyes and inspire, as you follow Dandelion's courageous journey. *Badass Abroad* gives a behind the scenes view of real-life transformation, the work you have to put in to make it happen, and the benefits of doing it."

Sundae Bean
Transformation Facilitator and Podcast Host of *In Transit*

"Relatable and funny, Claire Hauxwell weaves together her own experiences and insights in this engaging memoir showcasing the challenging reality of life as an accompanying spouse. If you've ever told yourself that you have nothing to complain about in your expat life (even though you secretly feel like something is missing), then you don't want to miss this book. It's sure to help you feel less alone, more empowered, and perhaps even inspire you to embark on your own journey of discovering your missing piece."

Melissa Parks, PhD
Mindset Coach for Entrepreneurs (formerly a coach and therapist for expats)

BADASS ABROAD

HOW TO GET YOUR
EXPAT SHIFT TOGETHER

CLAIRE HAUXWELL

First published in Great Britain by Springtime Books

© Claire Hauxwell, 2022

All rights reserved. No part of this publication may be reproduced, stored in or introduced into a retrieval system or transmitted, in any form, or by any means (electronic, mechanical, photocopying, recording or otherwise) without the prior written permission from the publisher.

This book is sold subject to the condition that it shall not, by way of trade or otherwise, be lent, resold, hired out or otherwise circulated without the publisher's prior consent in any form of binding or cover other than in which it is published and without a similar condition including this condition being imposed on the subsequent purchaser.

ISBN: 978-1-9196133-4-5

Design by Creationbooth.com

Disclaimer
Names, characters, places, and incidents are either the product of the author's imagination or are used fictitiously. Any resemblance to actual persons, living or dead, events, or locations is entirely coincidental.

To my daughters, I hope you always chase your passions and test your limits… just like you test mine. Don't let anyone, including your own head, hold you back from being the very best version
of you.

"A mother who radiates self-love and self-acceptance actually vaccinates her daughter against low self-esteem."
— Naomi Wolf

And to my husband, thanks for never saying no to the things I need to do. You seem to get me when I don't get myself.

"She knew she loved him when 'home' went from being a place to being a person."
— E. Leventhal

Contents

	A letter to the reader	1
1	Excuse the rumors – let me introduce myself	3
2	I'm fine. It's fine. Everything is fine.	15
3	What (and I can't stress this enough) the fuck?	31
4	Me: I'm finally happy. Life: LOL. Wait a sec…	49
5	I meant to say it… just not out loud	63
6	That moment when you realize this *is* your circus and those *are* your monkeys	77
7	"I told you so…" Sincerely, Your Intuition	93
8	My brain has too many tabs open, and I can't figure out where the music is coming from	107
9	You can't make everyone happy – you are not tequila	123
10	My alone time is for everyone's safety	135
11	Being married is like having a best friend who doesn't hear anything you say	149
12	True friends say good things behind your back and bad things to your face	161
13	My life is one big IDK	179
14	Your work is not your worth	193
15	Your new life is going to cost you your old one	211
	Epilogue	225
	Acknowledgments	229
	About the author	231

A letter to the reader

Hey there,

I'm so glad you decided to take a chance on me by picking up this book. There's a high probability you're currently an expat, getting ready to embark on your first overseas assignment, or toying with the idea of moving abroad. If so, these pages were written specifically with you in mind, and I hope they'll help guide you down your own personal path of badassery.

The story of our main character, Dandelion, is deeply personal. She is me and I am her. The chapters you are about to read contain MY personal story of transformation. I wrote it in the third person because it was easier for me to write the hard stuff as if it happened to someone else. Think of Dandelion as a new friend. One who's been around the block, and maybe like you, has experienced a lot of similarly shitty scenarios. Obviously, no two journeys are the same, but if you're anything like Dandelion and me, you'll find comfort in knowing you're not alone in the way you feel or how you've reacted to the universe's way of pushing you out of your comfort zone. Besides, life is hard, and you know how misery loves company… and a good glass of wine.

I chose to name the characters of this book after things found in nature, mostly flowers and trees, to disguise the identity of the people they are based on. They are a mishmash of personas from my past. I didn't just throw any old name out there but genuinely tried to match the character to the name. I know, it's a bit quirky. But hey, it's my book.

I believe each of us deserves to be the best version of ourselves. For a long time, I didn't know what this looked like. The image of my 'best version of me' faded somewhere between having children, leaving my career, and creating a life overseas. My entire sense of identity shifted from being a financially independent working momma to an overwhelmed stay-at-home mom of two who wasn't allowed to open her own bank account. Along with my identity went my confidence and my idea of fulfillment – I didn't know who I was. Ultimately, these pieces of my existence became so uncomfortable that I could no longer accept the way they made me feel. So I finally got off my ass and did something about it.

As you read these pages, you'll notice each chapter ends with a #MyTheory section. Every theory includes nuggets of wisdom and perspective gained during my expat life, along with an offering of tips and tricks that work for me. Please keep in mind that I don't have everything figured out; nor do I claim to. This is my story – the steps I took to change the trajectory of my life and the tools that helped me keep the momentum going. Take from it what you will. You should also know, Dandie and I will never be done blooming.

I already know just how amazing you are, my friend. I'm here to nudge you into finding this fact out for yourself. And I know you; a badass never backs down from a challenge.

Big love,

Claire

1

Excuse the rumors – let me introduce myself

#Dandelion

I told you I could do it

"See, Daddy. I can do it myself," declares the little girl with long pigtails. "I can fix it."

Her father is quietly observing his daughter pry a lug nut off the training wheels of her bike. Dandelion has always had a knack for tinkering and taking things apart in her daddy's workshop. She's also determined to conquer riding a two-wheeler bike before the annual 4th of July bike parade in her neighborhood. Her father promised he'd buy her a new bike once she learned, and she has her eye on a sweet purple cruiser with a banana seat. She already knows how she wants to decorate her ride in red, white, and blue.

"Okay, Dandelion, you let me know if you want any help," offers her father, and he goes back to putzing around his workshop.

Ten minutes later the bike is free of its training wheels and twenty minutes after that Dandelion is flying down the boulevard with her pigtails blowing in the wind like the ears of a joyriding dog with its head hanging out a car window.

She squeals, "I told you I could do it, Daddy!" as she proudly rides past him, smiling.

***

"Again," demands her instructor. "It's close, Dandelion. But it's not perfect."

The tired teenager has been rehearsing endlessly to perfect the set of *fouettés* for her role as the Lilac Fairy in the ballet *The Sleeping Beauty*. She is frustrated and annoyed. She knows she can do it, so she keeps trying again, and again, and again. Still not hitting the mark, her instructor says, "Maybe it's time to stop for tonight. You look exhausted, and it's getting late."

"I can do it," insists Dandelion. The sweat is dripping off her and the windows of the dance studio are steamy with annoyance and dedication.

"Let's not push it. You can try again tomorrow." Her instructor tries to coerce her star pupil into taking off her ballet slippers for the evening.

Dandelion's got tears in her eyes and blisters on her feet, and her ego is feeling deflated by pesky pirouettes. "No. I can do it. Let me try one more time," she says with a little too much assertion. Her instructor reluctantly nods in agreement and turns to cue the music. Dandelion shakes her arms and legs out, taps her toe boxes, and prepares for the music to begin one last time.

"*Pas de bourrée* and one," she counts in her head, her arms opening and closing, her head snapping, and her leg flicking the air to the beat of the music. Sixteen turns later, Dandelion finishes with a double *pirouette* and a smirk across her face. "I told you I could do it."

***

Jerry, a sales exec, sits across from Dandelion in a Sales and Operations Planning meeting on a warm Wednesday afternoon and condescendingly asks, "The plant has been up and down for maintenance issues all quarter, but they're saying their issues are behind them now. Dandelion, do you actually think you can manage to change the operation to run the most optimized schedule to cover our targeted sales forecast?"

Dandelion replies without looking up from her spreadsheet. "I can make it happen. I wouldn't have offered to do it if I didn't think it was possible." She doesn't look up from her spreadsheet to see his response and thinks, *No, Jerry... I'm just saying it for shits and giggles.* The meeting ends and Dandelion overhears the team of sales execs mocking the efforts of the operations team as she heads back to her office. *Typical.*

Weeks later she sits in the same boring Sales and Operations meeting with the same pompous sales exec. He sheepishly admits his failure: "We missed our original sales target this quarter. I doubted we'd be able to hit our production goal this quarter based on poor past performance, so I pushed the sales to next quarter and didn't update the operations forecast. Who knew we could hit the original target? Now we've got extra inventory we need to off-load and no open orders because of diverted sales."

From her burgundy swivel office chair, Dandelion soundlessly murmurs, "I knew, Jerry. I told you I could do it."

***

Sitting in her cramped Swiss kitchen feeding a snack to her two-year-old daughter, Thistle, Dandelion is trying to wrap her head around what she could make for dinner. After only two months of living in Geneva, she is feeling the effects of missing home and is craving comfort foods. *Mom's meatloaf, mashed potatoes, and green beans – sounds perfect.* "That's easy. I can do that," she says to the refrigerator.

With her list in hand, she gathers her seven-month-pregnant self together, hands Thistle over to her husband, Oak, and heads out to the grocery store, making sure to pee one more time before she leaves the house. After parking her car and squeezing her torpedo-sized belly between her Volvo and the car next to her, she walks confidently into the store. This time she even remembers her own reusable shopping bags.

She strolls up and down the aisles, quickly gathering items from her list – ground beef, eggs, yellow onion, green beans, potatoes, cream, and butter. Her last item was breadcrumbs. "Hmmm, where the hell do you think they keep the breadcrumbs?" Dandelion keeps repeating to herself as she tries all the places she'd usually assume they'd be hiding. Having had no luck of her own, she finally realizes it's time to ask for help. In terrible broken French, she shyly asks a clerk, "*Pardon. Où puis-je trouver de la miettes de pain?*" This loosely means, "*Excuse me. Can you tell me where the breadcrumbs are located?*" It probably sounded as terrible as you just imagined and is apparently incorrect. Looking as if he's been asked to move a piano up a flight of stairs, the annoyed clerk brings her to the flour aisle. "*Merci,*" she responds and woefully goes looking around the store again.

Dandelion finds a female customer who looks kind and asks, "*Pardon. Où puis-je trouver de la miettes de pain?*"

The nice young woman brings her right back to the same flour section.

"*Merci,*" Dandelion says as tears begin to stream down her face. There in the baking aisle, the woman who could always do whatever she put her mind to sits crying over goddamned breadcrumbs.

The sheer madness of breadcrumbs getting the best of her does not settle well with this very hormonal and moody mama to be. She wipes away the snot and tears to find herself being stared at by the other shoppers. *Nothing to see here, people. Just a good ol' American* **#hotmess**.

Dandelion grips her shopping basket and heads to the bakery section, where she grabs the biggest baguette she can find. If she can't find breadcrumbs, she'll just have to make them herself. She checks out as fast as she can, avoiding all eye contact with other shoppers and clerks – she's positive they're talking about her on the store's loudspeaker. *Beware of the crazy lady who keeps asking for flour in the baking aisle.*

Once she is home, Dandelion cranks the oven temperature up, shoves the baguette in, and slams the door shut. A while later she pulls the hard bread from the oven to cool and finds a plastic zipper bag and a meat mallet. She breaks the bread into large chunks, places them in the bag, and proceeds to beat the shit out of the baguette with the mallet until she has a pile of what looks like sand. *Et voilà,* breadcrumbs.

Sixty minutes later dinner is served – meatloaf with mashed potatoes and green beans. As she plates her family's meals, she says to herself, *I told you I could do it.* Years later she learns the French translation for breadcrumbs is *chapelure*. Not that it matters; she never chooses to buy them again.

If she were a flower, she'd be a DAMNdelion

Our heroine, Dandelion, is a *#badass*, though she isn't aware of it. She is funny, smart, kind, helpful, independent, determined, cynical, and sarcastic. She occasionally has *#restingbitchface*, but that's not her fault because it's a medical condition. There is research on this topic, and maybe 'frequently' is a better word to use than occasionally. She is an *#ambivert* – half introvert and half extrovert. This too is a thing. She loves to be surrounded by people she knows well, is shy when she's overwhelmed by strangers, and can definitely hole up in her bed alone with Netflix without issue.

She's quite the ASS

Dandelion has a lot of on-the-ground experience living abroad. She's been a *#ASS* – Accompanying Supporting Spouse – to a corporate executive for over a decade in five different countries. She's certainly been an ass in a lot of other life situations, but she's actually proud of being this kind of ASS. Dandelion often tells herself that her husband either married the right woman or a really dumb one. Not many women would be able to handle the stress and instability of packing up and moving their total existence from country to country every few years. *#expatlife* is not for the faint of heart.

This chick has been around the block a few times. She's American-born but has put down roots in five US states and five international locations on three different continents – Geneva and Zug, Switzerland (same country, but completely different cultures and languages); Brussels, Belgium; Mexico City, Mexico; and Johannesburg, South Africa.

This girl is a moving pro. From pre-move prepping, like clearing out the closets and selling off random crap online via the local expat group (which by the way is a total racket and pain in the ass… "Yes, I'd love to sell you my $400 stand mixer for your shitty low-ball offer of $20") to managing the loading and unloading of a container on her own in the dark on the side of the road and then living in a sea of paper and boxes when the container arrives six to twelve weeks later. Dandelion can manage the process blindfolded with one hand tied behind her back.

Not only does she get the family moved from one place to another, but she also does all the shitty grunt work like collecting the necessary documents to submit for visas, researching schools, and figuring out how to get her dogs from one continent to another. Dandelion finds the horseback riding schools, the swim lessons, the pediatrician, and the pet sitter. She is the *#magicmaker* for her family. She doesn't get a salary; she works like a mule and basically goes unnoticed to the untrained eye. Non-expats think her life is rainbows and lollipops with a gin and tonic kicker. Those people couldn't be more wrong.

Her husband has an awesome wife

Dandelion met her husband, Oak, while she was still in college. She's been with him longer than she's been without him. He is a funny and laid-back guy who makes her life better just for being part of it. And even though Dandelion sometimes wears a hard exterior, when it comes to Oak, she's a softie and couldn't imagine being on her life adventure with anyone else. He's always quick with a joke to make her smile or a smart remark to break the tension.

Oak works harder and smarter than anyone she's ever met. Besides her of course. He puts in long hours and travels a great deal, so, unfortunately, he misses out on a lot of their family's daily life, but he does his best to be there when she needs him, and she appreciates the extra effort. Dandelion can't recall how many birthdays and anniversaries Oak has missed over their 20 years of being together, but she knows he'd rather be with her and their family than in a crummy hotel room in India.

He depends on Dandelion to be the stabilizing pillar of their family – supporting him, their children, and their global life. Without her, there is no way he can do what he does so well. Her role as an ASS is probably the single most important part of his expat existence. If Dandelion isn't doing a happy dance about expat life, Oak's work performance is at risk. Happy wife, happy life. So he and his company have a lot riding on her ability to easily transition each time her life is uprooted and replanted in a new place.

Her nickname is Mom, but her full name is Mom Mom Mom Mom…

Together, Dandelion and Oak are raising two very spirited daughters, Thistle and Wild Violet (AKA Wivi). Neither of them has ever really lived in their passport country, but shockingly sound very American. They speak a couple of languages and Dandelion is convinced one day they will have a language of their own that they can openly speak in front of her, and she will have no clue as to what demonic plan is being developed right under her own nose.

This dynamic duo has weathered more transition in their short lives than many people will encounter in a lifetime. Dandelion and Oak often question whether they are royally screwing up their kids or raising highly malleable global citizens. These Third Culture Kids easily slide into new schools and activities with not so much as a pause to take a deep breath before entering their new world. They make friends easily, can converse with adults, and love to travel. Maybe their parents are doing okay after all.

Thistle looks just like Dandelion. There is no denying this child. She is a carefree kid who like her mom walks to the beat of her own drum. Dandelion sometimes wishes she could get her cadence in sync with Thistle's because they tend to battle like rams on a Swiss mountainside. She is a spitfire who will one day be a master negotiator for hostage situations. She fights for her personal causes with vigor and doesn't take no for an answer. She is an 'ask for forgiveness later' kind of girl who ultimately has a heart of gold and more empathy than anyone Dandelion has ever met. She's your typical tween – moody and dramatic – and her favorite saying is **#whatever**.

Wild Violet is the spitting image of her father, with a funny demeanor and a voice for belting out the tunes. Her imagination and creativity are way beyond her years. Wivi is a passionate young lady, though sometimes this passion of hers lands her in trouble because she's not willing to compromise. But realistically, who is? Like her personality, she's got a colorful sense of style – think 'gets dressed in the dark' – and owns it like a runway model. Wivi is a social butterfly who is master at using her charm to get what she wants but can still throw a tantrum like an overtired toddler.

Soulmates aren't just lovers

Dandelion is also a fierce friend. She adores her tribe of special women. Her soul sisters are more than just trusted comrades, they are steadying forces of strength scattered across continents and separated by oceans. At any time of the day, whenever she needs to lean on someone, Dandelion knows there will be an ear to bend. They are her *#anchors* when she is weathering a storm of inconceivable quandaries and personal dilemmas. Never doubt the ability of these women, as they are a force to be reckoned with.

Having been badly burned by friendship, Dandelion has become a bit guarded and more particular about who she lets enter her friend zone. Please don't be offended if you need to give her some time to loosen up and trust. She most likely wants to be your friend, but she won't be offended if you don't want to be hers in return. And that's okay. She's still going to do her best to be nice to you because karma has the revenge tactics of a jaded woman.

Keep it simple, stupid

Our brave girl, Dandelion, is probably a lot more things, but in all honesty, she's a simple human. She loves her family, her friends, and her dogs. She enjoys adventure but keeps to a schedule for her sanity. She sweats at the gym in lieu of therapy sessions – though sees nothing wrong with therapy and has benefited from it personally in the past. And she knows when it's time to recharge her batteries because she craves the sun on her face and the sand between her toes. She will make you a killer margarita when you are at your wit's end or a lasagna for your family when you can't make one yourself. She's an everyday girl who loves jeans and t-shirts and will welcome you into her home if you ever need a place to escape.

Ms. Fixit

As you can tell from the description, Dandelion is more than a little independent and determined – which are good and bad traits. It's SO good because she's totally capable of slam-dunking any task thrown at her. She's not afraid to roll up her sleeves and put in some hard work to get the job done right. No matter how big of a soup sandwich she is trying to wrangle. It's also SO bad because Dandelion hates to be part of a sinking ship and always seems to think it should be her personal mission to help right the boat. This is both kind and annoying. Let's face it, she's not a miracle worker. Or is she?

Dandelion has found herself trying to be the real-life expat version of Kerry Washington's portrayal of Olivia Pope in the TV series *Scandal* – a modern-day *#fixer* of all things gone awry. Though she's yet to cover up a murder. She manages to figure out how to order heating oil, get the tumble dryer fixed, eradicate the house of pigeon infestations, and deals with a stack of bills each month that need to be paid in multiple countries – all while trying to speak a different language. And don't forget she does the shopping, the vacation planning, the cooking of most meals, and runs a taxi and laundry service, as well as a full-service wellness program that includes everything from making doctor appointments to the submission of insurance claims – without batting a lash.

With no hesitation and wearing a smile – or is it a snarl? – she lovingly jumps on the *#lifegrenades* her family lobs at her daily. You need black shoes for tonight's band concert? On it. You said you'd bring 24 cupcakes with red and white frosting for the bake sale at school tomorrow? No stress. A dinner party for 16 of your staff later this week at our house? You got it, honey.

Wonder Woman seems to be what she's striving to be. And from the outside looking in, you might think she's wearing a gold-detailed bustier and metal cuffs under her t-shirt and jeans. Trust me, she's not – but her husband might think that sounds kinda cool. Instead, she's a woman who questions herself, sacrifices her sanity for the sake of others, and wishes she could just get a good night's sleep occasionally.

Dandelion's a mom who worries about whether she's royally fucking up her kids by digging up their roots and replanting them so many times. It's challenging for her to watch her kids cope with growing up in today's world when all she wants to do is swoop in and help. She knows that won't teach them how to be fearless street-smart women who aren't afraid to get dirty and don't have to depend on others for what they can do themselves. But she also wants them to have an arsenal of tools at their disposal, including the ability to ask for help, and be empowered to deploy them when needed. The struggle is real because *#parentingishard*.

Sweet Dandelion is also a loving wife who behind the veil of a smile sometimes feels resentful and unappreciated. The sacrifices she's made for his career have been hard to swallow at times, but she's hopeful those twinges of pain will eventually pay off. *Bring on retirement!* No, her marriage isn't perfect, but whose is? Never having to doubt the strength of the bond she and Oak share is comforting. Even though she lacks confidence in other parts of her life, she undoubtedly knows her husband will support her if she just stops being afraid to tell him how she really feels.

There's no doubt Dandelion lives a good life – some might say it's charmed. She doesn't feel like complaining is an option because she wants for nothing, and even though she yearns for *something*, she tells herself, "It's fine." Trying to lean into the idea of accepting that she's "just a mom" or a "trailing spouse" puts her at odds with who she used to be. There's an itch she can't seem to scratch and it's beginning to really piss her off.

#MYTHEORY

The comedian George Carlin once said, "I like it when a flower or a little tuft of grass grows through a crack in the concrete. It's so fuckin' heroic." I've always loved Carlin for his ability to discuss taboo topics and use the word fuck so eloquently. I feel like even though we wouldn't have seen eye to eye on every topic, we would have been friends if our paths had ever crossed.

When I envision Carlin's image of a little flower, I imagine Dandelion. She's a tough little cookie. Even in the harshest of conditions, Dandelion is resilient and will find a way to bloom. She gives a bit of beauty to a not so pretty space. She spreads kindness with her cottonlike seeds and hopes others will bloom bright because of the impact she has had on them. Dandelion often doubts her ability to be beautiful and feels like she might shrivel in the scorching unsheltered heat of the summer, but she is refreshed by the rains of remembrance – recalling how she's always managed to make the best of a situation, learned from it, and bettered herself for the experience.

I think there is a bit of Dandelion in every single one of us. Each of us has a version of her waiting to take root into the soil of life that isn't always seen as conducive to thriving. The time it takes to make those roots hearty and viable varies from person to person. We all take a different route to our destination, and in the end, we hopefully find ourselves in full bloom by showing the world our dazzling colors, our distinct shapes, and our delightful fragrances.

In a world full of roses, I'd rather be a dandelion. Let's face it, roses are fragile and delicate, need near-constant attention, and can only thrive in perfectly pH-balanced soil. They may be pretty, but they are incredibly high maintenance.

Dandelions aren't sissies, are hard to kill, and are great at blooming just about anywhere — then they let the wind take them to the next phase of their life to continue to grow bigger and better.

I think George was right; that flower is fucking heroic.

2

I'm fine. It's fine. Everything is fine.

#fine

Fine is a four-letter word

One thing you must know about Dandelion is that she loves a good four-letter word. They can be useful in any situation – good, bad, happy, sad – and the tone is key to their multifunction. For her, the word *#fine* is no different. Maybe that's why people say learning English is so damn hard.

For example, the phrase "I am *fine*." Are you really fine, or are you passive-aggressively baiting your spouse into an argument? Are you really fine, or are you hiding a hot mess of emotions because you don't want anyone to know you're struggling? Are you really fine, or are you just accepting the status quo? It all depends on the tone.

As a person who's a wildly independent people-pleasing perfectionist who doesn't like to fail [whoa… hello, high-functioning anxiety!], Dandelion has used the word fine countless times to keep the conversation moving without getting into the hairy details. After a decade of living abroad, she's become much too aware of the use of the word fine. The word fine has been used in some of the worst – and best – drivel Dandelion has ever heard spewed by an ASS who simultaneously painted a big fat smile on her face. She is 100% guilty of using it too.

She believes the word fine is camouflage for the truth ASSes are too scared to say out loud. They are apprehensive about how their partners might react or worried their friends and family will think they are failures. An ASS doesn't want to hear, "I need you to figure this out because my career is at stake," or, "I told you it was a bad idea to move overseas." An ASS also doesn't want to admit they are struggling, confess to being lonely, or concede they find living abroad the hardest thing they have ever done. And don't forget, they don't want to admit how extremely homesick, frustrated, and resentful they sometimes feel while living a life that others could only dream of.

Dandelion thinks that's bullshit.

Dandelion doesn't like that she pees her pants when she does jumping jacks but has announced it publicly so often – in front of complete strangers – that you'd think she's fucking proud of it. She's no longer afraid or ashamed to admit her truths. At some point in her expat life, she has been every single one of those things – frustrated, lonely, homesick, resentful. You name it, she's felt it. She only wishes it hadn't taken her all these years to be strong enough to admit her feelings out loud. Life isn't an endless parade of unicorns like the carefully curated Facebook and Instagram feeds she scrolls through each day. Her life may be flawed, but at least it's real and is no longer just *fine*.

Yes, I'm FINE – Freaked out, Insecure, Nervous, and Emotional

At the beginning of Dandelion's expat life in Geneva, she was drowning. That's not a joke. She felt like a disaster. But as time passed she began to get her sea legs, and by the time her ship landed in Johannesburg eight years later, she could have been captaining the boat. But she wasn't.

Our ASS unknowingly gained a lot of life experience with each international move – you know, the kind of stuff that can't be taught in school. Every place she replanted herself had its challenges, and each time she found herself with a new issue dropped in her lap, she did what she does best – she put her head down and overcame it. Dandie never actually failed at anything when it came to expat living; she just wasn't always doing it to the level she'd become accustomed to. Or was it some unattainable standard that she'd put on herself? And somehow, the confidence she once had went into hiding, with her identity riding shotgun.

    If you had to pick one trait to describe Dandelion, it would have to be resilience. She's a doer, someone who doesn't give up when things get hard and isn't afraid to get dirty to get the job done. She just needed a reminder of who she already was – a badass abroad.

***

In 2009, Dandelion and her family made their first overseas move – to Geneva. She was seven months pregnant with a very active two-year-old and a workaholic husband. The phrase "it's not a good time" is annoying because it's never a good time. But moving overseas at seven months pregnant may not have been a good time.

    She didn't remotely look like she had her shit together because it was literally scattered around her as if Thistle had dumped her Legos on the living room floor. She was on an emotional rollercoaster of hormones, exhaustion, and loneliness. Well crap… that explains why she felt like people were staring at her. Sometimes self-reflection is a mean mirror.

    But you know what? Being a disaster was okay because she was doing the best she could. She had a lot going on and controlled the chaos to the best of her ability. She wasn't *fine*, but realistically who was going to notice but her?

***

After six months in Geneva, Dandelion had only made a couple of friends, Pansy and Hyacinth. They'd finally segued from coffee after baby gym classes to Sauvignon Blanc in the garden during playdates. They were also juggling overseas life, newborns, and distracted husbands. Playdates were full of boobs, babies, and blankies. Each dealing with their own struggles, these friendships were still fresh, and Dandie didn't want to scare them off by unleashing her crazy train from the station. She thought these women were open to listening to her psychobabble, but she wasn't sure she could be 100% honest with them about her feelings yet – how she didn't feel like she was **#killingit** as a new mom in a new country with a new language. Come to think of it, she wasn't being honest with herself.

"I can't figure out how to get this kid to latch on," admitted Pansy. "He just sits there and gnaws on my nipple. It hurts, and it takes eons for him to feed. I don't have time to sit on the sofa feeding him for hours on end while my daughter runs around like a lunatic. Plus, I think I'm losing my milk supply." She traced the rim of her wine glass with her beautifully manicured finger. "Ugh. I feel helpless."

Whoa. Pansy was pretty ballsy to admit that, thought Dandelion while she sat quietly listening to the conversation bounce around her. *I guess I feel that way too sometimes. However, I'd never say it out loud.*

"Have you tried a lactation consultant?" asked Hyacinth. She took a quick sip of her wine before plucking her phone out of her exquisite-looking handbag to scroll through her contacts to find the consultant she used. "Mine helped me a lot. Let me give you her number."

"What about you, Dandelion?" asked Pansy. "How are you doing now that Wivi has arrived? Does she take forever to eat?"

Dandie looked down at her baby sleeping in her car seat, then glanced up at her toddler running around the late summer garden. It was warm, and she felt tired. Wivi was a good eater, too good, really. She had her mother up every three hours to feed, and by the end of the day, the plump little flower child would lose her damn mind because her over-milked momma had been sucked dry from feeding her all day long. Sounding a bit deflated – kinda like her boobs – Dandie finally replied. "I'm *fine*. She's a good eater. I'm lucky I can turn an episode of *Dora* on to keep Thistle distracted long enough for me to get Wivi fed and changed. I can't complain." [The hell you can't.]

She wasn't lying, but she certainly wasn't letting her guard down to show the cracks in her foundation. She didn't know why she hid the truth. That was a lie, she knew exactly why – feeding her baby was one of the only things that seemed to be working for her lately. Her house resembled a tornado's aftermath, she needed a haircut badly, and she didn't feel like she was adjusting to life in Geneva at all – but she had a fat little baby who was a champion eater. So, of course, that's what she admitted. She just wanted everyone to know she was doing something right.

"I'm jealous," Pansy confessed. "Share your secret with me."

Hahaha. Sorry, but who's this woman trying to kid? Her friend looked as if she'd come to their backyard playdate straight off the runway of a summer collection fashion show, with a flawless face and perfect tresses, and she was dressed in a beautiful vintage-inspired sundress. Dandelion was lucky to be wearing clean clothes, and her cracked cuticles hadn't seen a manicurist in months. She wasn't quite sure what was making her feel so fucking inadequate; maybe she felt like a tarnished version of who she used to be.

"My midwife told me fennel tea is helpful with milk supply, so I drink a ton of it, even though it tastes terrible. You should give it a try," she offered her polished friend. Dandelion hid her unkempt nails under the table.

***

The following year, Oak made another career move, and their family relocated from Geneva to Brussels. Wivi was now a toddling 16-month-old, Thistle was a rambunctious three-year-old, and Oak traveled 85% of the time. The same shit show, just a different city. But in Brussels, Thistle began attending the international school. Being part of a diverse school community eventually became a **#gamechanger** for Dandelion. She now had an opportunity to meet other ASSes – it was like she'd hit the jackpot of potential mom friends.

While standing in front of the large bubbling fish tank in the lobby of the elementary school, Dandelion was in the middle of having a meltdown moment. It was only the third day of school for Thistle, and Dandelion was feeling drained from the container arriving the week before. Her toddler was being a challenge. It was only 9 a.m. and Dandelion was already trying to rally herself to get through the rest of the day. She sat Wivi in front of the glowing blue box of colorful fish to give herself a minute to regroup.

Two breezy-looking women strode over to her. "Hi!" said one of them. "How are you? We're Zinnia and Viola. Is everything alright? You look like maybe you could use a coffee. Would you like to join us?"

"Thanks, but I'm *fine*. I just need a minute to get myself in order," blurted Dandelion without looking them in the eye. She probably even added some excuse for why she was scrolling through her phone, having finally managed to detach her daughter from her leg for 90 seconds of freedom.

It's like her shame response was prerecorded and ready to be engaged on command. [WTF, Dandelion, you are so much better than that!] She knew that by saying "I'm *fine*," the conversation would continue and no one would dwell on her sorry state. It was safe. Fortunately, the sunny duo saw right through her fake *fine* façade and insisted they grab that coffee. She can't be sure, but she later recalled one of them taking Wivi from her arms to make sure Dandelion didn't try to run away.

This chance meeting changed the trajectory of Dandelion's expat life. Having two total strangers, who later became her friends, see through her sham of a response and insist on her joining them for coffee was proof that a really shitty morning could turn into a great day when you stopped being so worried about what others were thinking and accepted a little bit of kindness even when it was hard.

***

Dandelion examined an empty bedroom that faced a front courtyard covered with amethyst-colored petals from a canopy of jacaranda trees. It was May 2013. She walked over to the window to take in the view. Peering through the electrified fence wrapped in barbed wire that encompassed the housing compound, she watched a steady pace of cars making their trek from one side of Mexico City to the other. *I bet this place is noisy*, she thought, and then tried to pry open the window. She eyed a considerable amount of water damage on the windowsill before successfully getting the window ajar. A rumble of traffic noise immediately assaulted her as if someone had suddenly turned up the volume on a radio.

"What do you think of the house, *señora?*" asked a young relocation agent with alarming red lipstick. "*Es bueno, no?*" She was holding a folio full of papers and was focused on her phone again. The phone had had the agent's attention all day, and Dandelion didn't really feel like the cardinal-lipped go-between gave two shits for what she thought about the house.

Oak walked into the room and stood next to his wife. He looked out the window to figure out what had caught Dandelion's eye. "What are you looking at?"

"The electrified razor fence wrapped in barbed wire."

"Wow," he said. "I guess we're not in Kansas anymore, eh?" The Sofía Vergara wannabe left the room to take another phone call, and Oak quietly continued. "I'm sure it's got adequate security," he said, eyeballing the guard shack. "We knew what we were getting into when we accepted a transfer here from Brussels." He paused. "It seems like a nice enough house even if the location isn't the greatest. Don't you think?" He wasn't looking at her as he spoke.

I hate to break it to you, Oak, but 'adequate' and 'nice enough' aren't exactly phrases one gets excited about when moving into a new home.

Dandelion felt pressured to like this house because it was the last one on their short catalog of available properties, and it would be nice to tick this to-do off the list. There was a long pause before Dandelion finally answered her husband. "It's *fine*. We'll make it work." She knew she was settling again and was already trying to figure out a way of gerrymandering her life into this less than perfect place.

Here we go again

"Where did you say you moved from?" interrogates the perky Petunia during the new parent coffee morning on the first day of school. Behind the frizzy-haired woman hangs a banner that reads: "Back to School BBQ – September 10, 2016."

"Mexico City," responds Dandelion. Now on her fourth expat assignment, Dandelion knows exactly what to expect at these sorts of events.

"Right," follows up Petunia. "And how are you settling into life in Johannesburg?"

"Ugh, *fine*... good?!? Great. Everything is going just *fine*, thanks," replies the exasperated and coiffed – because you don't show up to these things looking like you just rolled out of bed – Dandelion, who also resembles a teary-eyed deer in headlights with a bogus grin. But hell, she is still moving, and like it or not, she is still *fine*.

Petunia sees Dandelion as a duck – coolly keeping her shit together on the surface but paddling like hell below, and she's also fresh volunteer meat.

"Oh, I'm so glad," chirps Petunia, gently patting Dandelion's arm. "Seriously, you just let me know if there's anything I can help you with, okay? Here's my phone number. Call me anytime." Petunia isn't insincere with her offer of help, nor is she kidding about signing Dandelion up for volunteering. She's just heard it before and knows exactly what *fine* means because she's been there and done that.

"Thank you. That's very kind of you," says Dandie. She knows off the bat she isn't going to call her but doesn't need to let her know that. The Joburg **#newbie** isn't that green and already knows exactly who she's dealing with – the self-appointed leader of the school parenting world, the PTA President.

Someone or something behind Dandelion catches Petunia's attention. "I'm so sorry, will you excuse me?" she says and quickly saunters off to engage with her next target. As PTA Petunia walks away, she looks back over her shoulder and says, "Oh, and Dandelion, don't forget to sign up to volunteer for this year's PTA events. It's a great way to get involved!"

Petunia is right. Dandelion is holding her shit together the best she can. So is every other ASS out there who's in a similar situation. Even though she is a veteran expat, Dandelion is currently a newbie – and that means she feels super vulnerable. She most definitely needs help with some random things such as where she can find gluten-free, sugar-free, soy-free fruit snacks for her picky eater, but she's too embarrassed to ask. Dandelion is appreciative of the ceremonial welcome, and as she walks over to the volunteer sign-up table, is undoubtedly a *#sucker*.

I love that I don't have to act socially acceptable around you

A few months after settling into the daily grind of life in Johannesburg, Dandelion finds herself in what seems to be a very good place. One thing she admits is that life in Johannesburg is easier to navigate purely based on language. She no longer stumbles over her words to get her point across and always gets what she expects when ordering food at a restaurant. Except when she tries the local delicacies like impala or kudu with monkey gland sauce.

Making friends in South Africa comes easy to Dandelion. She's not sure what she did to be so lucky this time around, but she isn't taking this little *#lifeperk* for granted. Finding new friends every few years is exhausting. So stumbling upon a fabulous group of women who happen to be her kind of people is a saving grace.

A woman by the name of Rosemary, who Dandelion only knew from online interaction, sets her up on a blind friend-date with Canada's version of Marilyn Monroe – without the red lipstick and beauty mark – named Dahlia. She's dressed casually in a jean skirt, tank top, and sandals, but Dandie picks up an artsy vibe from her handcrafted copper bangles and talk of an art exhibit in Joburg's CBD. And who's kidding who? Their lunch date is more like an interview. Dahlia is lovely, but Dandelion understands this friend-making process well and intentionally drops a well-placed f-bomb to test her date's reaction. Let's face it, one must cut to the chase much quicker when you're an expat with limited time to figure out if you like each other and want to play nice. Dandelion is met with an f-bomb response from her lunch date, confirming their compatibility.

The friendship treaty is stamped with a seal of approval from both parties, and Dahlia welcomes Dandelion into her everyday world, where she meets Rosemary (Rosey for short) in real life and not via instant messenger. Rosey is an energetic Aussie with a thick accent that Dandie has to learn to decipher over time – it's like going back to language school. Rosey has a tell it like it is mentality and doesn't take any bullshit. Her hair is shaved on one side of her head and her biceps look like she's implanted oranges into them. These ladies become part of Dandelion's new normal. A few months later, Magnolia (AKA Mags), Rosey's cool, calm, and collected confidant, who's quick with a snarky comment and always sporting pink lips, moves from Mexico City to Johannesburg and completes Dandelion's tiny posse of friends.

This group of women complement one another, each bringing something different to their unique friendship. Dandelion genuinely feels as though she belongs to this badass lady-tribe who empower and support each other without judgment. No longer does she feel the need to shelter her friends from the crazy thoughts tumbling around in her mind; instead, Dandie willingly shares the issues that are stressing her out and making her feel like a total nut job. It's safe to say she's in good company because the things they say make her feel sane.

Having a community of trusted friends she can depend on makes the feeling of being detached from family and friends back home a little easier. If there's an emergency, she isn't worried about who to call. They don't judge her even when she looks like hell and really needs a shower. They're a supportive group of friends who genuinely care for one another's wellbeing. When one friend ghosts the rest of the group, the perpetrator is dropped in on, called, and texted till they answer. They collectively pitch in to help a stressed-out mate when they can't do it alone, and they never forget to laugh through the tears they shed because life is easier when you share the load with those who understand you. Dandelion's grateful for this little gang of strong and smart badass women, and she cherishes their friendship.

Fine is an F-word, but so is fulfilled

For years, Dandelion witnesses herself and other ASSes repeatedly settle for being *fine*. Figuring out how to use the power of *fine* lets her control her narrative. *Fine* immediately deflects unwanted attention when she feels inadequate or just doesn't have the energy to get into it.

Totally aware of what she's doing, Dandelion isn't proud of her tactic. Knowing she's been using *fine* for far too long, she tries to stop herself from overusing it. Hell, she continually wills herself to say "I'm having a hard time" instead of tossing out "I'm fine," but dodging bullets on a bad day is sometimes the easiest way out. Hey, no one is perfect and bad habits die hard.

Discussions about the phenomenon of *fine* have often been had by Dandie and her expat girlfriends over the years, and the theme is always the same: life is pretty good, but *something* is missing. That *something* is a bit of an enigma; a lot of ASSes feel its absence but can't quite identify what it is.

"I really am *fine*, and happy too. But **#something** is missing. I can't put my finger on what it is," Rosey confesses one night as they sip their sundowners during a girl's getaway weekend deep in the South African grasslands. The group of women speak softly as a dazzle of giraffes crosses the valley below their rooftop perch.

"I know. I feel that way too," says Dahlia, crossing the room to refill her drink at the bar. "I'm content. I have a good life, and I shouldn't really complain because I'm so **#blessed**. But I just feel like there's a piece of me missing."

Blessed, shmessed. Maybe Dandelion isn't feeling like a badass lately, but claiming to be blessed isn't the answer for her. The sky's searing hues of deep orange and purple fascinate Dandelion as she watches the sun fade slowly under the horizon. She's simultaneously processing what her friends have just said. She too feels like *something* is AWOL in her life. Is she happy? Sure. Does she have a good life? Certainly. Is it okay for her to complain even though she has a unique lifestyle that allows for an abundance of opportunity? Abso-fucking-lutely. She lives a privileged life, but that doesn't mean she can't gripe on occasion like any other human being. Her emotional needs still require attention, and when they are starved of a bit of recognition, she feels lost, down, bored, meh, bitchy, grumpy – or fucking *fine*. After a decade of expat reality under her belt, it hits her. She is *fine*, and she is happy, but she isn't **#fulfilled**.

"I mean, I used to have a job," groans Rosey. "One that paid me good money. Where people used to praise me for a job well done. Now

I'm just everyone's personal assistant. I'll admit life was more difficult when we lived in Vietnam, but nonetheless, no one acknowledges how hard I work. I just wish—"

Without regard for anyone speaking, Dandie cuts Rosey off mid-sentence. "Do you feel *fulfilled*?" At first, the faces of her friends look at her like she has three heads, but they eventually realize she is serious, and Dandie continues. "I feel *fulfilled* in certain parts of my life, but not at all in others."

After a moment of silence, Dahlia pipes up. "Yeah. Yes. Yes!" The rest of the ladies begin nodding their heads in agreement. "Dandelion, I think you are onto *something*."

That night Dandelion lies in bed staring at the star-studded sky. She can hear lions in the distance and wonders exactly how far they are from her door and what she should do if they come through the window. She feels as if her thoughts and emotions are feeding on the menacing roar of the lions. She knows she has a good life with a loving family and caring friends, but one vague and obscure part is missing – *something*. She realizes her *something* is a sense of fulfillment outside of being a wife, mother, and friend.

Many aspects of Dandelion's expat life have been dictated by other people. She's been told where she's going to move, what language she's going to learn, and what cultural norms she's expected to live by. Like many ASSes, her family is the single thing she can truly influence, and she gladly spends much of her energy nurturing it. But still, *something* is missing, and she's the only one who can figure out what the hell it is.

#MYTHEORY

Awkward doesn't even scratch the surface when trying to put into words how it feels to unexpectedly uncover *something* about yourself that you didn't even know was negatively affecting you. I certainly had no idea I was feeling so unfulfilled because I was so busy trying to make sure my people were thriving, and for fuck's sake, I was *fine*.

Fine is a polished version of *okay*. Who craves being *okay*? Not me. It just took me a little while to admit that to myself. Covering up our real feelings with a terrible masking expression is just a lie. This may be the genesis of my distaste for the frigging word *fine*.

Never do anything you wouldn't want to explain to the paramedics

Before I go any further, I want to clarify a few things because I feel like some people might have their knickers in a twist about the idea of being unfulfilled and mixing it up with being ungrateful.

1. **One can be grateful and not be fulfilled – it's that simple.**
   Feeling fulfilled has nothing to do with gratefulness. I was very grateful. I knew damn well I had a splendid life and felt guilty for complaining at the same time – but that doesn't change how I felt. By accepting being unfulfilled, I gave myself permission to seek out what was missing, not permission to be a twat.

   Being someone who gives themselves (time, energy, productivity, etc.) to others can create joy for the giver. Who doesn't like to see a smile on another person's face because of something they've done? But it doesn't always mean the giver's internal needs are being met. I don't think this makes the giver ungrateful for the joy they do have in their life, it just is what it is – a missing puzzle piece. On the flip side, you can seem fulfilled and be ungrateful, but this means you probably have a questionable value system and are a bit of a self-centered jerk. I'm not a psychologist, but I think I might be right.

2. **ASSes sacrifice enormously to help their spouses succeed — period.**
One of the main reasons my husband is so damn successful is because of me. For all the years he's been an expat, I've been behind the scenes pulling strings like a puppet master while making significant sacrifices. Yes, my husband might physically change his place of work, but for the most part, his life doesn't change too much — he gets up, goes to work, and comes home.

ASSes, on the other hand, must literally cut off their old lives and start a completely new one. They give up their entire sense of normalcy — their jobs, their families, their homes, their friends, their favorite restaurant, even their favorite exercise class, AND they possibly repeat the process every two to five years. So please, spare me, but don't tell me ASSes are ungrateful.

3. **Fulfillment doesn't have to come solely from giving to others — duh.**
Fulfillment can come in many forms. I think a lot of people believe being fulfilled is being busy. No way, José. I was more active than ever when I discovered my unfulfillment. The resentment I felt for all the stuff sucking the life from me should have been a red flag.

Maybe you like sitting on your porch cross-stitching while drinking lemonade — if that helps fulfill your needs, awesome. Keep that shit up. If you love to cross-stitch but can't find time to do it because you are always doing other stuff, you aren't fulfilling your need. It's pretty basic math in my opinion. I'd say you need to figure out a way to sit your ass back down and start stitching your heart out again. I can't be 100% sure about this, but I think this is where ASSes begin to lose their identity. We stop fulfilling our wants and needs, and eventually we forget what we used to enjoy and what defined us.

When I visualize my version of *something*, I imagine a group of empty microscopic cells floating throughout my body. The cells circle my body, pulsing through my veins, and like a thief in the night, they snatch a bit here and there as they endlessly travel from my fingers to my toes and back up to my brain, which refuses to stop overthinking everything. The tiny cells don't ever swipe a large enough piece of my existence for me to visually see a void. Only when the fragments are gathered and pieced together like a jigsaw puzzle do I realize what a significant piece of me is missing.

Do something today that your future self will thank you for

I look at it this way: you've got a choice to be *fine* or to be *fulfilled*. But hey, maybe you are already fulfilled, and if so, double high five to you. I hope you are celebrating that accomplishment, my friend. But if you aren't and you feel an inkling of *something* missing, please don't ignore it. You're the only one who can recognize the need for action. Who cares if you don't know what the *something* signaling you is? Here's your chance to find out. Your *something* is sending out a rescue beacon. You can either ignore it and bury it deep in the dark at the back of your mind – where let's be realistic it will gnaw at you – or you can throw it a life preserver and breathe life back into it until you are both floating in fulfillment.

I don't think anyone should settle for *fine*. We all deserve much more than we think we do, and we're much more capable than we give ourselves credit. Dig deep and don't stop till you find the origin of your *something*. And when you find it, forge a new path to being whole. If you already know you are missing *something* specific, act as fast as you can to replace it. Don't waste years fumbling around. If you don't know what that *something* is, don't be afraid to seek out guidance from someone whose job it is to help you find your path, such as a coach, mentor, or counselor, like I did.

Making a commitment to work with a coach was one of the best choices I ever made for myself. My journey to collaborating with a coach has a bit more meat to it, and we'll get into that in the next chapter, but man... if I'd had the tools to keep me from going down that pothole-riddled path to Shitsville, I'd have been kicking the ass of expat life a long time ago.

I wish I had been told it was okay to not be *fine* years ago. I can't even fathom where life might have taken me if I'd been privy to this little tidbit of info. So listen to my words and embrace the challenge... *something* is waiting for you. Now get off your rump and go find it.

3

What (and I can't stress this enough) the fuck?

#WTF

There were plenty of signs

Her first encounter with Oleander is on the phone.

"The people here seem so, I don't know… blue collar. Wouldn't you agree?" These are the words Oleander uses to describe the locals she met at a happy hour with her husband and a few of his colleagues and their partners. It's the first time Oleander has socialized since moving to Johannesburg a couple of weeks earlier.

"Well, ugh. No," is all Dandelion can think of saying. *#WTF is this woman jabbering on about?* She wonders if Oleander stirs her coffee with a silver spoon. Who says things like that – especially on the phone with someone you've never even met? It bothers Dandelion so much she later mentions it to Mags to get her reaction, and she too is unimpressed. The "blue collar" thing should've put a nail in the coffin of this potential friendship for Dandelion, but sadly our heroine's instincts are caught in a blind spot.

Rosey once told Dandelion, "You're always trying to find the good in people. And I love that, but sometimes you try so hard searching for the good that you miss the bad." This is one of those times. Instead of being Oleander's friend, she should continue to be kind at arm's length. [Dammit, Dandelion, you don't have to be buddies with everyone.] She ignores the signs to steer clear of this relationship because she's a kind and welcoming person. This is a

#bigmistake. Dandie knows she doesn't need more friends, but she also knows what it's like to be a lonely newbie and that a simple act of kindness can change one's outlook. Maybe blue collar is a term of endearment back in Boston. But Dandelion wasn't born yesterday.

Pay close attention to those who don't clap when you win

Once the unlikely pair become friendly, Dandelion feels a sense of unfettered freeness. Oleander isn't afraid to be a little crazy and daring. She has an enormous amount of confidence, and she can fill a room with laughter. She's fun, engaging to be around, and makes others feel good – unless you are the subject of one of her gossipy cock-and-bull stories, which tend to be spot on. She's the kind of person who goes out of her way to make you feel important. Or so Dandelion thinks.

"Come on Dandelion, you've got time for one more glass of Veuve before you leave," Oleander says enticingly. "We're worth it," she says with a wry smile as she fills Dandelion's flute with bubbly. "Did I tell you what happened at lunch the other day with Poppy?"

Oleander has a way of making you feel like you're the center of her world. What Dandelion doesn't know is that Oleander does this with everyone. Getting them on her good side is the easy part; keeping them there is the tricky bit.

Dandelion has no idea Oleander is playing her like a cheap fiddle. Her new friend can tell a great story and draws Dandelion into them like a skilled fisherman with a prawn on his hook, and this makes Dandelion wriggle with a kind of complicity. Back home later and nursing a headache, Dandelion unpicks the tall tales, questions Oleander's motives, and finishes up giving her the benefit of the doubt. And yes, you've guessed it, Oleander is floating the same types of stories about Dandelion to others, but here's the shitty part: she tells Dandelion what others have been saying about her – all of it bullshit. And even if it isn't, why does she care so much? Sadly, Dandelion falls for these lies hook, line, and sinker. Her pride kicks in, and she reacts poorly by joining the rumor mill chitchat and throwing her own grenades of gossip.

"You're kidding, right? She said that about you?" says Dahlia. "I don't believe it for a minute." Dahlia's baking a cake for her daughter's birthday, and Dandie is helping decorate by being there for moral support.

"Why would Oleander lie?" counters Dandie. "I mean, it's so childish." Dandelion can't wrap her head around the idea of Oleander flat out lying to her.

"It is," says Dahlia, "and that's what makes me question why Poppy would say such a thing." She's spreading white buttercream over a round triple-tiered layer cake filled with raspberry jam. "I don't know Poppy very well, but she doesn't seem like the kind of person to say something like that. If it's true, I'm stunned." [OMG, Dandie, listen to your friend! Stop making excuses.]

Dandelion also starts to pick up on Oleander's one-upmanship mentality. If someone says they won the state championship for badminton in high school, Oleander would have won the state championship and got a full-ride scholarship to the best school in the nation for it.

Dandelion writes a blog – *The Bloom Chronicles*. For many years it's been a way of staying connected with family and friends back home, but over time, writing has become more of a passion. The blog has morphed into an expression of thought about her expat experience and is an outlet for creativity. No longer are Mom, Dad, and Aunt Gladiola the only ones reading it. She's reaching people all over the world and really hitting a chord with her readers.

At lunch one day, Dandelion tells Oleander about the goals she'd set herself before turning 40 in a few months. "I'm trying to test my writing skills a bit," Dandelion starts, "by submitting pitches to a few different websites and magazines. I'm not holding my breath, but it would be pretty cool if one accepted my idea."

"Uh-huh." Her lunch mate is scrolling through her phone and doesn't seem to be paying any attention to her.

Dandelion continues. "I was also contacted by an old Brussels friend who encouraged me to apply for a writing position with Global Life." GL is an organization that focuses their work on individuals who live abroad and the complex issues that accompany it. Each year

GL selects a handful of writers to document their annual conference. Dandelion had applied but again hadn't given it much thought after pressing the send button. "If I get selected, I'll get to go to the conference in Singapore."

"Yeah? That's cool." Her lunch mate finally stops pecking at her phone and looks up at her. "Did I tell you the ladies' club liked my idea about organizing a golf tournament for the women's shelter? It's going to be amazing." Oleander continues to speak, but Dandelion stops listening.

Whenever Dandelion talks about her writing with Oleander, she initially feels like she's going to be praised for her work, but her accomplishments are quickly swept under the rug by whatever bigger and better thing Oleander is currently cooking up. This makes Dandelion feel like whatever she's done isn't good enough or deserving of praise. Most of Oleander's grandiose ideas never come to fruition anyway, but that doesn't matter because whatever Dandelion has going on is now forgotten, like a lost sock in the laundry.

What's left unsaid says it all

As with most relationships, Oleander's sparkle begins to fade. Even though Dandelion is still ignorant of her new friend's web of lies, she finds herself, like most of the others, becoming immune to Oleander's crazy-making.

"It's not my fault she missed it," says Oleander, referring to her daughter missing a rehearsal for an upcoming gymnastics showcase. "The teacher never told me it was mandatory."

Of course it isn't your fault, thinks Dandelion. *Even though the teacher sent an email to all parents last week with the subject line: Mandatory Dress Rehearsal.* Dandelion can't be bothered to prove Oleander wrong. She's sure the email is sitting unread in Oleander's inbox.

"This teacher really needs to get her act together or I'm not reenrolling her for another session," threatens the muddled mom.

Be careful what you wish for, Oleander. The teacher just might appreciate that gesture.

There's always some sort of modern-day tragedy unfolding around Oleander, with her at the center of the drama. Dandelion begins to question Oleander's intentions and little by little starts to pull away.

At the same time, Dandie notices more and more comments about Oleander's lack of consideration for others.

"Hey, Dandie, have you seen Oleander?" asks one of the trainers at the gym as Dandelion scans her membership card and walks through the turnstile. "She's late for her personal training session with me again."

Um, nope. Wasn't my turn to watch her.

How is she to know why Oleander is late or a no-show? She too is tired of chasing or waiting on her and tired of listening to her daily dramatic interpretation of life. It's all becoming a bit much. Isn't her time just as valuable as Oleander's? Like every ASS, Dandelion's dealing with enough crap of her own and no longer has the desire or capacity to keep up. This doesn't mean she doesn't value their friendship, but Oleander is turning into a Venus flytrap. A kind of energy vampire who's draining her emotional stamina and eating her alive. Dandelion's feeling suffocated by their bond and needs some space.

Dandelion never mentions any of this to Oleander because she knows discussing the way she feels about their friendship will veer their relationship off course and it won't end well. [Um, hello, Captain Obvious here… this is another enormous red flag! Dandelion, you don't worry about how your real friends will react to your genuine concerns.]

When one of the Chatty Cactuses from PTA Petunia's posse – a prickly bunch of well-meaning do-gooders – confronts Oleander about flaking on her volunteer duties [god knows we all want to skip them, but don't because we aren't assholes] there is a huge scene at school pick-up. It is painful to watch Oleander rip into one of the Cactuses after they had the gall to confront her. Somehow Oleander manages to flip the situation – one of her clutch maneuvers – and makes it look like she's been the one who's been wronged.

Why is Dandelion investing so much into a relationship that is clearly not serving her? Too bad she doesn't have the balls to speak up about how she's feeling – maybe things would have played out very differently. Dandelion is tiptoeing around this friendship like she's afraid to poke a bear.

Now I understand why Peter Pan didn't want to grow up

Days pass and Dandelion forgets about her goals because she's too busy trying to casually distance herself from Oleander. [Because that never looks obvious.] This is easy to do when you don't think anyone is going to respond to your writing submissions, and well, you don't think they're important enough. Dandie gets on with her life and dismisses the idea that writing can be anything more than a hobby.

A few weeks before her birthday, Dandelion and Mags are at school counting tickets for an upcoming fundraiser. It's mind-numbing work, but it goes by quickly as the friends chat away. They're discussing Dandie's upcoming birthday party – the guestlist, the booze, and the dress code. Oak has put Magnolia in charge of planning a party to celebrate Dandelion's upcoming big four-oh. The party planner is not offering a single detail about the affair except that it's a 'white party.' Dandelion hates this idea.

"Why did you choose a white party? I hate wearing all white. Everyone hates wearing all white. This isn't Brazil on New Year's Eve." Dandelion isn't afraid of complaining to Magnolia, and Mags isn't afraid of telling her friend to get bent. She is the surrogate older sister Dandelion never had. They both grew up outside of Detroit, lived in two expat postings together (which is rare), and know the other would always be there for them.

"Because I wanted to," says Magnolia. This is all she offers up as a defense under the brim of her navy-blue baseball cap that is camouflaging her makeup-free face. Her ice-blue eyes are still dazzling, even without the help of shadow and mascara. Dandelion knows Magnolia has her best intentions in mind and that she shouldn't worry.

"I still think everyone is going to hate you for making them dress in all white."

"I don't care if they do." Magnolia possesses a 'no more shits to give' kind of attitude and a heart of absolute gold. She's the kind of woman who gives until she can't give any more and then figures out a way to squeeze out a little extra. She's a real badass who's been an expat for longer than Dandelion, and in some pretty gnarly places. It's always a good laugh listening to her tell stories of her times in a far-off land. "So, how do you feel about turning 40?"

"Eh, it's *fine*," answers Dandelion as she pushes tickets around in a fishbowl. "My first 40 years have definitely been a good ride." It may have been a good ride, but Dandelion's pretty sure it's too late for her goals to come to fruition.

"But," jabs Magnolia.

"But when I imagined myself turning 40, I never thought I would be just a housewife."

"And there it is."

"There what is?"

"Your resentment."

"I'm not resentful." Dandelion pauses to gather her thoughts. "I'm just nostalgic for a career." This last sentence sounds more like a question than a statement.

"A career, huh? And what kind of career are you nostalgic for exactly?" Magnolia isn't holding back. She's Dandelion's senior by 15 years. Even though they're in the same expat lifeboat, they're at different phases of their lives.

"I have no idea."

"You want to get up and go to work every day on top of all the other shit you've gotta do? Friend, I'm not buying it. What's the real reason you think you need to go out and get a job?"

"Remember when I talked about *something* missing at our girls' weekend?" Dandelion reminds her.

"Yeah."

"I still feel like *something's* missing from my life. I wake up and do the same thing every fucking day. It's not very fulfilling." Dandelion counts out ten raffle tickets and rips them from a spool before tossing them in a pile. "What's going to happen when I wake up one day and I have no kids to take care of and I'm stuck living in Timbuctoo while Oak's at work all day?"

"I know you don't see it, but you have a lot on your plate," says Magnolia. "I feel this way too sometimes. Your feelings are valid. But I don't think a nine to five is going to fill the void you've got brewing in you. I'm just worried that you are trying to be someone that you really don't want to be because that's who everyone else thinks you should be." Magnolia is being sincere and Dandelion can sense her concern.

"I just miss the idea of using my brain."

"I'm pretty sure you used your brain when you put on an entire kids' carnival at school. I know you used your brain the other night during fifth-grade math homework. Your brain was ready to implode when you were submitting the international health insurance claims you were complaining about to me the other morning. And I'm positive you used your brain when you helped your gardener apply for asylum."

Dandelion hadn't seen it, but damn if Mags wasn't right. She *is* using her brain; she just doesn't view her efforts as critical. It's going to take a huge shift to rectify this massive oversight in Dandelion's mindset.

Please cancel my subscription to your issues

Over the next month, Dandelion does her best to continue to subtly put space between her and Oleander. No matter how hard you try to break up with someone without them knowing, it inevitably blows up in your face. Her overvalued friendship with Oleander abruptly ends and gets nasty like an infection.

Her *friend* used her kindness, then broke her trust. Unearthing the stories Oleander's been peddling about her – and hearing the original versions of the fabricated ones she'd previously heard about others – nearly does Dandelion's head in. As each piece of the puzzle finds its home in the big picture, Dandelion becomes more aware of the bizarro world Oleander has manufactured.

What gets to D the most is feeling like a fool for playing right into Oleander's hand. Dandelion knows she's acted like a complete bitch by retaliating with such harsh words to what Poppy had supposedly said about her. But Poppy was another one caught up in Oleander's snare.

She is appalled and disappointed by her judgment and her behavior. There's nothing in this world that Dandelion regrets more than believing Oleander's lies and trusting her with her private – though clearly influenced – thoughts. She summons the courage to apologize to Poppy for the terrible things she's said maliciously. This small action sparks a friendship between Poppy and Dandelion that should have existed from the beginning had there not been any outside influence.

Dandelion, Poppy, and anyone else in Oleander's path of destruction are just pawns in her game of control. Dandie's ashamed of herself, and it sours her stomach to think she ever trusted the woman. Putting space between Oleander and herself didn't seem to do as much good as Dandelion had hoped, and Oleander forces her hand into finally having it out.

It's a tense scene in a cheerful café when Dandelion meets Oleander face to face about everything she's discovered. She orders a mimosa – light on the OJ – to calm her nerves. Smoke and mirrors no longer plague Dandelion's vision, but she's aware there's no winning against Oleander's firm grip on bending reality and her inability to agree to disagree. Kiss up or shut up is Oleander's game, and Dandelion isn't willing to play anymore. [You can do this, Dandie.]

"You like control. You like to control every aspect of your life," spits Oleander. [Well, duh. Who doesn't like to try and control their own life?] "I'm so done defending you to others. Did you know I constantly shield you because people think you're cold and unfriendly? But I won't be doing that anymore. Maybe they were right. I thought we were friends. I thought you valued our friendship." [There it is, Dandie, her clutch move. Don't take the bait.]

Dandelion does or did value their friendship and is upset they can no longer be friends. She's hurt by the accusations Oleander's made. [They're lies, Dandie. This is part of her game. Don't listen to her.] It doesn't take long for Oleander to make her move to reverse the situation and lay all the blame on Dandelion. The prey knows it is coming and sits waiting for it to happen.

Sometimes a person needs to know when to walk away from irreparable relationships, and toxic friendships are no different. While listening to Oleander blabber on, Dandelion opens her wallet and pulls out some cash. She slips it under the bill, then places her wallet back in her purse. She looks at Oleander and says, "It's fair to say we aren't going to see eye to eye on this, and I just don't see any point in dragging this out any longer." Her hands are trembling under the table. Her last bit of confidence is waning, and the sadness and hurt can be seen in the tears welling up in her eyes. She stands to leave. "Blame me for whatever you want. At least one of us will know the truth." Dandelion's never felt so upended by a person who she considered to be a friend.

For a while, Dandelion thinks she can push through the emotional letdown, but she's too wounded. She would do just about anything to evaporate Oleander from her existence. Instead, she can't shake her – it's like having stepped in a sticky wad of chewing gum. You know, really fucking annoying. She's not interested in rehashing or resolving the situation. Dandelion – who's not struggling from selective toxic amnesia – would be dead if she cared any less. She's not able to change Oleander's outrageous behavior and shouldn't have to subject herself to her crap, but knowing this doesn't make the pain any less.

Dandelion just wants to move on without Oleander turning up around every corner of her little world. From the gym to school to the grocery store and anywhere in between, Oleander is there because expats live in the *#expatbubble*. Think six degrees of Kevin Bacon – everyone knows everyone, or someone they know knows them and their business. She feels Oleander's stares from across the room and the tension in the niceties they're forced to offer up in public spaces. It's uncomfortable and Dandelion knows Oleander knows just how it makes her cringe on the inside. And it feels like Oleander is relishing it.

If your dreams don't scare you, they're too small

Two weeks before her 40th birthday, Dandelion receives two emails. One from an online magazine editor interested in the article idea she pitched, and another from a woman by the name of Hawthorn offering her a writing position for GL.

Dandelion can't believe what she is reading, so she reads it again and again and again. If Dandelion is going to use one word to describe how she feels that morning, it's astonishment. Not in her wildest dreams did she think either of the little goals she privately set for herself would pan out. Someone chose her from a list of candidates. Someone had seen potential in her idea. Maybe turning 40 isn't going to be so bad after all.

Even though Dandelion is totally chuffed with herself, she doesn't tell a soul. Not her friends, not her parents, not even her husband. The goals had merely been a test. Now, real people are going to be reading what she writes, and actual people are going to be meeting her and seeing her in a professional setting. She is scared shitless by the idea of being put in the arena, and she contemplates withdrawing her name altogether. [WTF, Dandelion? You're kicking some serious ass!]

This attempt at self-sabotage is a joke. Dandelion clearly wants to prove to herself that she can achieve something more than being a chauffeur and short-order cook to her children. It's as if she set those goals to see if she still had it, like an athlete that comes out of retirement to prove to everyone they're not a has-been. It's basic bullshit, and if she doesn't allow herself to follow through with these goals, then she really is a has-been.

Luckily, our heroine gently removes her head from her ass and accepts the writing position and writes the article for the online magazine. Remember, she hates to disappoint people, even people she doesn't know.

As a writer for GL, she must work with a group of aspiring writers and authors to chronicle the conference. Dandelion is honored to be selected but feels entirely out of her league.

A prerequisite for being part of the writers' group is to complete an online course with the program's director, Hawthorn, and the other writers. Under the sunny South African sky, Dandelion plows through writing assignments while hadedas squawk overhead like small pterodactyls. Dandelion loves the writing and works hard to produce worthy pages for Hawthorn, who seems to like Dandelion's style – which is encouraging – and is always sending her positive feedback. Dandelion struggles with accepting the idea of people liking the words she strings together and usually shrugs off the compliments as people being polite. Hawthorn, in fact, is never 'just polite.' Dandelion fears her lack of confidence is seeping into her writing.

Dandelion is intimidated by the world of GL. It seems like many of the other writers are familiar with each other, and she feels like an outsider. Dandelion doesn't feel as though she is connecting with the group and is assuming her laid back and rough around the edges demeanor isn't what this crowd is into. She's afraid to speak up during class for fear of making a fool of herself. Why is she so hung up on what people think of her?

It's amazing how fast someone can become a stranger

Living in a small expat bubble makes it harder to dodge sightings of those who make your blood boil. But if she's honest, Dandelion also feels like she's in a weird state of mourning. Instead of having a laugh in the middle of the supermarket with her friend, she is skipping the cereal aisle to avoid her adversary.

And she just can't stop thinking about Oleander's comment. It felt like a dagger in her back. "People think you're cold and unfriendly." Was that true? It couldn't be. She isn't a cold person, and she definitely feels like she always tries to be kind. But why would someone say that? [To fuck with your head, duh.] She can't stop second-guessing every conversation she has each day – *Is this one of the people who thinks I'm an asshole?*

The final straw is when Dandelion receives a phone call from Daisy. Daisy is a friend in the expat bubble. Not a close friend but the nicest person you know, literally the kindest person in the world – who finds the upside to every shitty situation. So when you piss her off or she gets bad vibes, you know it's bad.

"You're on speakerphone, and there are kids in the car," says Daisy, "but this can't wait. You need to watch your back because she's digging for dirt on you. It's like she's plotting to take you down."

Let's just say it's a good thing Daisy warns Dandelion about the speakerphone – because she's furious. [By the way, Dandelion should never be on speakerphone.] Dandelion has no one to blame but herself. If she'd only trusted her gut during that first conversation with Oleander when she felt prickly behind the neck from her judgmental crap, this whole mess would've been avoided. But nope. Dandelion ignored the neon warning sign and is paying dearly for it.

The sudden weirdness is becoming apparent in her house too.

"Mom, why don't you hang out with Oleander anymore?" asks Thistle.

She doesn't think "because she's an asshole" is the best response to an 11-year-old girl, so she does her best to cover up the situation. "Oh, our schedules are just off lately," or, "She's got other plans tonight." When she does run into Oleander, it is utterly *#awkward*. Dandelion deserves a goddam Emmy for these performances. If Dandie's kids play with Oleander's on the neighborhood playground, Dandelion doesn't discourage it but certainly doesn't prompt the interactions. One thing for sure is that Dandelion doesn't want to put her children in the middle of her adulthood schoolyard drama.

Oak, the sensible man that he is, distances himself from the situation as much as possible and urges his wife to do the same. [Dude, she's trying.] As issues arise, he talks her off the ledge. Before she jumps off. He knows how much Oleander's actions have hurt his wife, and he's told Dandie how much it frustrates him.

"D, my advice is to let nature take its course," advises Oak one morning before work. "Stop stoking the fire, no matter how hard it is to avoid her. She's seeking out attention – good or bad, it doesn't matter. Ignoring her will infuriate her, but it sends a loud message. Oleander's true colors will bleed out naturally, and you won't be the one with blood on your hands."

She hates it when he sounds so smart.

Keeping herself distracted from the noise of Oleander's one-man band is nearly impossible. But with encouragement from her husband, Dandelion is determined to keep the crazy at bay and focus on what's ahead – the GL conference. She's been working hard preparing for it and can't let outside influences sidetrack her when she's nearly at the finish line. Besides, she's no longer alone in her battle of wills. It doesn't take long for a group of others to figure out Oleander's game too. One by one, the pawns take back the board, leaving a trail of wreckage in their path.

#MYTHEORY

Relationships are a significant element of my expat life. I know from experience that it can take a single connection to make life abroad better. I'm also fully aware that it can take just one to make it worse.

I've been extremely lucky in the creation of local and global groups of expats and badasses who are truly my kind of people. But I've also encountered characters that have made my life very challenging. This is completely normal – annoying but normal. Not everyone you meet will be your best friend, or hell, even like you. And that's okay. Sounds a bit harsh, but it's true.

Creating a community abroad is important and something of high value, especially when there's a longing for a robust group of people who can be relied upon when you're so far away from home. This strong desire for connection can sometimes blind us from seeing people for who they really are and what's actually going on – until it's too late. Which is exactly what happened to me.

Where attention goes, energy flows

I have a serious character flaw: I'm a complete sucker for wanting to find the good in people, even when I know deep in my soul that it's a bad idea. It's unfortunate, but not everyone has our best interests at heart. So I've had to learn to deal with toxic (negative or uber-positive) people the hard way — by confronting them head-on.

Had I been schooled in how to identify a crazymaker, I would've been able to steer clear of all the drama that comes with them. I mean, I'm glad I persevered and came out stronger on the other side, but I really don't want to ever go down that rabbit hole again. These days, I'm much more aware of other people's actions, whether they're directed at me or not. The actions don't always have to be directed at you for you to decipher their intent.

Here are some clues to when you might be dealing with a shit stirrer.

1. **They are total drama queens**
   Crazymakers always find themselves in the middle of dramatic situations. It's as if they are attracted to the attention (good or bad) and must share their story with anyone who will listen and help stoke the fire.

2. **Anything you can do, they can do better**
   No matter the topic, a crazymaker will continually one-up you. It doesn't matter if you've accomplished something great or are dealing with a tragedy, they'll always have a better or worse story to top yours.

3. **"I'm sorry, but..." is their favorite excuse**
   From consistently being late to getting caught talking behind your back, they'll never admit their blunders.

Crazymakers are infallible. Their noticeable pattern of excuses will never incriminate them when being honest and up-front could make everything better. Remember, inaction speaks louder than words.

4. **Intimidation is their weapon of choice**
Like a bully on a playground who makes life hell for their peers, a crazymaker who doesn't like what you're offering will try strong-arm tactics (including guilt and ultimatums) till they get their way. And like a bully, they typically do it because they know their use of coercion is uncomfortable and annoying.

5. **They love playing the role of martyr**
There's nothing like being told something along the lines of, "But I did that for you, and look what happened to me," especially when their input wasn't needed in the first place. This classic victim mentality is intended to make others feel they've put added stress or suffering on the crazymaker — when they're the one who actually created it.

6. **Give them a finger and they'll take the whole hand**
A crazymaker is great at taking advantage of other people's kindness because they're sure their target won't say no. They're shrewd at monopolizing people's time, they tend to over-communicate with excessive calling or texting, and they generally give off a co-dependent vibe.

I just asked myself if I'm crazy. We said no.

At the time, I didn't know how to deal with a Venus flytrap — I just kept feeding it till I couldn't take it any longer. I thought maybe I was the one who was losing my grip on reality. But I wasn't, and when I was wrong (and I was), I admitted it. The entire situation made me feel uneasy and still gives me shivers when I reflect on it. But that's what crazymakers do: they create chaos and relish it while others slowly go bonkers.

Being mad at myself was how I initially coped with being duped. The farce made me feel like such a joke, like I was inferior. This is something I no longer consider to be true, but when I was living through it – man, was it terrible. Coaching taught me how to cope with these kinds of relationships and how to prevent the situation from happening again. Hold tight because we'll get into that stuff later.

This might seem like an odd thing to say, but I guess I've been bitten one too many times. These days, I'm much fussier about who I choose to spend my time with. When I do decide to invest in a relationship, I'm much more observant. The natural back and forth of a relationship must even out with the ebb and flow of life. If there isn't the same level of reciprocation from the other person, it's a big turn off for me and sends the signal that the other person might be feeding off me. I don't think I'm being critical; rather, I'm making sure the relationship is benefiting both of us and not just the one benefiting from my tolerance.

4

Me: I'm finally happy.
Life: LOL. Wait a sec...

#thefuckening

It's OK. I'm on 500 mg of Fukitol.

As the conference approaches, Dandie gets a sense her nerve endings are on high alert. From dealing with the emotional letdown from Oleander to stressing about her lack of confidence in a professional setting, she feels crabby and short-tempered. She fears her professional skills will be dead on arrival after not being used in over a decade. Is she even capable of talking to the other attendees without making a total jackass of herself? Dandelion can take command of a PTA meeting full of Chatty Cactuses without any preparation but is meek in the face of personal development. Putting together a presentable wardrobe from her flip-flops, ripped jeans, and activewear is another struggle she's having to tackle. She's a colossal mess.

Oak is supportive about Dandelion going to Singapore, though her daughters aren't quite sure what to think.

"Why is Mom going on a business trip? She doesn't even have a job," is one of the mutterings Dandelion overhears between Thistle and Wivi. There's nothing quite like hearing your child say "Mom doesn't have a job." Talk about a blow to one's ego. Fortunately for Dandelion, Oak gets wind of this nonsense and lays into the girls a little.

"Your mother has the hardest job on the planet. She takes care of you both! She's been chasing the two of you your entire lives – she started off wiping your butts, and now she taxis you around like an Uber in waiting, and she doesn't even get a paycheck. Instead, she gets paid in whining, moaning, and unexpected problems to solve. For who? For you. And on top of making sure you two princesses don't wilt and die, she takes care of me, the dogs, and the house. She pays the bills, she buys the food, and she does it all out of love," belts Oak. "Your mom doesn't have a job? Ha! I can't wait till you two become mothers."

    She probably isn't supposed to hear the intense interaction between Oak and their daughters, but she's glad she did. It reassures her that even though the girls don't always know what she sacrifices for them, her husband sure as hell does. Glimpses of Oak's appreciation help wash away a bit of the hidden resentment that sometimes bubbles over when Dandelion doesn't feel an abundance of gratitude for her silent sacrifice.

    Of course, Oak is wrangled into a last-minute trip to New York City at the same time as Dandelion's trip. She is lucky to have a strong support network in South Africa and knows things are going to be fine with someone else running the show for a week. There's nothing more **#expatlife** than having your entire family dispersed over three continents unexpectedly.

    Dandelion is so appreciative of her **#anchors**, who step in to make sure she doesn't miss out on this opportunity. Before Dandelion leaves, she gathers up her **#ladytribe** for a pre-trip huddle at her house. All these special women help celebrate her success and send her off knowing she deserves this chance to shine.

    She packs her suitcase, grabs her laptop, a notebook, and a few pens, and thinks, *You can't back out now, so you'd better* **#putyourbiggirlpantson**. She is anxious but excited about this opportunity. Maybe it's going to be a turning point for her. Where it'll take her, she has no idea, but there's no stopping the momentum now.

    The entire Uber ride to O.R. Tambo Airport has Dandelion feeling jumpy. She checks to see if she has her passport ten times. Upon arrival she checks her bag and realizes Oak has upgraded her ticket to business class. *Sneaky*. She isn't used to traveling alone. No one to keep her eye on, no one to tell "Don't forget your backpack," and no one telling her at the last minute that they need to pee.

She walks into the business class lounge and scans the room and all the travelers. Most of them have their nose in a laptop and are talking into an earbud while they scarf down the buffet canapés and complementary beer and wine. Dandelion decides on a quiet spot in the corner, where she peacefully relishes her Sauvignon Blanc and reads her book. Another thing she isn't used to doing in an airport.

Her flight status flips from ON TIME to BOARDING on the TV monitor perched on the wall in Dandelion's cozy corner. She loads her belongings back into her carry-on bag and slips down the corridor to the gate with ease. *Flying without your family is a breeze*, she muses. Dandelion hands the gate attendant her boarding pass and passport, takes a deep breath, and boards the plane bound for Singapore.

Trust me... As you get to know me, I get weirder

As she approaches the check-in table in the brightly lit corridor of the hotel lobby, Dandelion hears a thick southern drawl. She can't be sure, but it sounds very Texan.

"Hey! Welcome to the Global Living conference," says the super excited woman from behind the table. She's wearing a blue dress and her hair looks like a sable stole. The woman is stunning yet totally approachable at the same time. Must be the familiar accent. She reminds Dandelion of a beauty queen.

"Uh. Hi! Thanks. My name is Dandelion Roote. I need to pick up my conference packet."

"Oh, an American. You sound like you're from the Midwest. Am I right?"

"Yep. Detroit," responds Dandelion with her nasally midwestern accent.

"Dallas," the woman says as she starts sifting through manila envelopes with white labels in the corners. "Rany, Rhan, Rinna... Roote. Found you." She looks up from her neatly organized table of envelopes and hands Dandelion the one with her name on it. "Oh gosh, where are my manners?" She sticks her hand out confidently toward Dandelion's and says, "My name's Amaryllis Johnson, but people call me Lis for short. It's nice to meet you, Dandelion." Amaryllis is a perfect name for this tall drink of Texan beauty.

"Thank you, Lis. It's nice to meet you too." Dandelion peeks in the envelope, pulls out her badge, and slips it around her neck.

"Oh! It looks like this is your first conference *and* you're a GL writer! How exciting. I look forward to reading your work. Have you written anything I might have read already?"

Dandelion is a bit taken aback by Lis' excitement. "Well, I write a blog called *The Bloom Chronicles*."

"Stop it. You do not."

"I promise you, I do." Dandelion isn't sure what else to say.

"Wait till I tell Myrtle you are here. She loves the way you write."

Stunned and exhausted, Dandelion can only think about getting into her room to recharge for a bit. "Well, I have to be going. It was nice meeting you, Lis."

Dandelion heads to her room, unpacks her suitcase, grabs a quick shower, and finishes readying herself for the day. She's to meet Hawthorn and the rest of the writers for lunch and there's a workshop scheduled for the afternoon to prep the team. While putting on her earrings, she examines herself in the mirror. *Are you ready for this, Dandelion Roote?* She slides some muted plum gloss across her lower lip and smacks her lips together. "I hope so because it's GO time."

Dandelion finds her way to the restaurant and opens the door. It's a small, unassuming place clearly known only by the locals.

Suddenly there's a slender man standing in front of a curtain that leads to the dining room. "Can I help you?"

"Yes. Hello. I'm meeting a group here for lunch. The reservation is under Hawthorn."

"Ah, yes. Please come with me. She's already here," says the man as he pushes aside the curtain and ushers Dandelion through the doorway.

At the back of the room is a large round table with ten chairs. All but one occupied. *For Christ's sake, am I late?* She glances down at her watch to check the time. She's five minutes early. *At least I don't have to decide where I'm going to sit.*

She approaches the table full of women and is greeted with a murmur of hellos.

Hawthorn stands up and comes around the table to introduce herself. "Hello, Dandelion. It's so nice to meet you. I hope you had a good flight and are settled into your room." Her British accent lilts over every word.

"It's a pleasure to meet you too. Yes, thanks. All settled and ready to get to work."

"Well, this week's not all about work, Dandelion. I do hope you'll have a bit of fun as well." Hawthorn looks around the table to see her lunchmates nodding in agreement. "GL is about making connections and experiencing life too."

"Right," says Dandelion, looking down at her feet.

"We've all just arrived ourselves, so let's get started with introductions." Hawthorn makes her way back to her chair and sits down. "I just want to let you know how excited I am to have you all on board for this year's GL writers' panel. We've got a diverse group that I'm sure will produce a wonderful conference book." Hawthorn looks around the table and then begins again. "Okay, so you all know me already. Dandelion, since you were our last arrival, you go first."

Fuck me. "Okay." She takes a deep breath and scans the table for a glimmer of connection before beginning. "Hi. I'm Dandelion Roote. I'm American and currently live in South Africa. I've been an expat for almost a decade, and I write a blog called *The Bloom Chronicles*. I'm very excited to be here and to get to know all of you." Dandelion is met with soft smiles. Everyone around the table looks nice, but will she fit in?

The extra baggage will cost you

The world of Global Living is an overwhelming experience for Dandelion. She finds herself surrounded by people she only knows from virtual interaction on social media. Some people recognize her.

One person even says, "Aren't you the woman who writes *The Bloom Chronicles*?"

"In the living flesh, I'm Dandelion Roote," she replies.

"Nice to meet you. I'm Sunflower," says the cheerful woman, who's being greeted by people from all angles. "Is this your first time at a GL conference? Isn't it amazing?"

The two chat for a few minutes and in that time at least five other people say hello to this woman named Sunflower before everyone's ushered into a keynote speech.

"It was great meeting you, Dandelion. I hope you enjoy the rest of the week," says Sunflower as they are separated by the swarm of people entering the hall. "I hope you'll check out the session I'm hosting tomorrow." The woman is immediately in conversation with another group of conference goers. Dandelion thinks she is the epitome of confidence.

During the workshops and talks, Dandelion meets a bevy of culturally diverse people with a passion for living abroad. Everyone she encounters seems so accomplished – from authors to artists, coaches to psychologists, and academics. Dandelion doesn't know how she fits into this community but thinks they're all sort of speaking the same expat language and are connected by similar experiences.

To help her concentrate, she sits in the front row of every session she's assigned to write about, but Dandelion's mind keeps drifting. *Good thing I'm covering my ass by audio recording every session on my phone. Am I fitting in? Does it matter? Am I sporting too much resting bitch face? Probably. Am I a good enough writer to be here? Hawthorn seems to think so. Why am I so fucking worried about what others think of me?*

This is the beginning of *#thefuckening*.

After attending sessions and networking the entire day, Dandelion is spent. Those things are extremely hard for this girl because she doesn't particularly enjoy big crowds and not knowing anyone. Her brain hurts. She's become acutely aware of how self-conscious she is about her deficient professional background, and she's overwhelmed by the idea of having to keep up this charade for the rest of the week.

The idea of attending happy hour doesn't sound appealing, but Dandelion goes anyway. She knows she must keep trying to put herself out there when all she wants to do is curl up in her bed, binge on room service, and watch Netflix.

"*Just one drink,*" she tells herself. God knows she could use one. Sipping on a vodka soda, she bounces like a pinball from one crowded area of the bar to another. She feels invisible and ends up finding herself holding the wall up like a nerdy seventh-grader at a middle school dance. After finishing her drink, she heads back to her hotel room with a belly full of knots.

Tears begin to well in her eyes as Dandelion inserts her key into the door. She tries to hold back tears of embarrassment and shame for thinking she'd be able to dupe everyone into believing she's something she isn't. What exactly is she trying to make people think anyway? She's nothing but a wannabe writer who doesn't have any credentials after her name. Infuriated with herself for getting into this mess, she doesn't know how she's going to make it through the week. She feels like a big fat **#imposter**.

No longer feeling *fine*, Dandelion spends the remainder of the conference in the shadows of the crowd. Before the conference, Dandelion felt like she'd gotten her **#shitshow** into a state of livable chaos. She knew her life wasn't perfect, but it sure as hell could've been a lot worse.

Now, with the plane sitting on the tarmac waiting to take off for Johannesburg as the rain drips from a gray sky, Dandelion finds herself feeling empty. She hoped this trip would empower her, but instead, she feels lost and unsure.

After replaying her interactions at the conference in her head, this teary-eyed woman sits in seat 15A, doubting herself. Hoping she didn't sound as inexperienced and unprofessional as she assumes she did, and wondering what kind of impression she made. Is it as transparent as she feels? She is so damn caught up worrying about what others think of her and whether she radiates the right image. [Dandelion's older and wiser self would have given her some sage advice at this point: get over yourself and just be you.]

I don't have anything to hide. But I don't have anything I feel like showing you, either.

"So, how was the conference?" asks Oak as they take their seats al fresco at their clubhouse.

"It was *fine*."

"Fine doesn't really sound like it was worth all the work you had to do to go," responds Oak. He is focused on placing his dinner napkin in his lap. His words feel like a gut punch.

"I'm just really tired from the flight and looking forward to snuggling up with the dogs later." She averts her eyes on purpose. She slips the wine list from the pile of menus and begins looking it over. She doesn't have to look at it because she knows every wine on the list.

A smiling waitress approaches the table. "Hi, Dandelion! How are you? Where've you been lately?"

"Hey, Jacaranda." Dandelion smiles back. "I was traveling last week. Glad to see you missed me."

"Let me guess, a big draft beer for you?" says Jacaranda, glancing at Oak, "and a Sauvignon Blanc for you, Dandelion?"

"You know us too well," Dandelion says as she slides the wine card back into the menu.

"Do the girls want an orange soda?"

Dandelion looks out over the balcony and can see the girls playing in the distance. "Yes, that'd be great. Thank you, Jacaranda."

The slender young woman walks to the bar, and the couple stay silent. Dandelion doesn't know why she doesn't feel comfortable confiding in her husband. It's probably because she's embarrassed about the way she feels, and if she says it out loud, it's admitting failure. Oak probably wouldn't have seen it that way, but Dandelion is too afraid to talk it out and find out his real reaction. Instead, she conjures up what she *thinks* he might say and believes that. [Way to put those awesome communication skills to work, Dandie.]

Once she's recovered from jetlag, life goes back to normal. Dandelion continues to struggle with her newly discovered imposter syndrome and confidence loss. These souvenir trinkets that unexpectedly slipped into her luggage make her angry and upset.

How the hell did a one-week trip to Singapore, something that was supposed to be fun and enlightening, turn into Pandora's box of wicked tricks?

All her pals bombard her with questions via their group chat, and Dandelion's responses couldn't be more *#vague* – "It went well… I learned a lot." She never openly speaks about the experience because she's afraid the truth might come out. That she felt like a big fat imposter and that her confidence had abandoned her at 30,000 feet. Even Oleander texts her to ask how the trip went – an attempt to engage with her – but Dandelion doesn't take the bait.

I hope rock bottom doesn't have a basement

For a couple of months, Dandelion is hyper-focused on cranking out her writing assignments for the Global Living book. She also volunteers a boatload at school with various activities and is prepping for the end of the school year. Her girls have birthday parties and events that need planning. She challenges herself to go to the gym six days a week to keep her sanity. Dinners, girls' nights, parties, and spa days fill her agenda. Keeping busy is Dandelion's coping mechanism. By always moving, she keeps herself distracted and manages to stifle that pesky feeling of being adrift. Dandelion understands that she's burning the candle at both ends.

She's also doing her best to duck and cover as Oleander declares war on the expat bubble. The woman is burning bridges left and right. It's just one calamity after another – from making a mammoth hullabaloo over her child's part in the school play to why she isn't invited to Poppy's birthday lunch. [Bet you can guess who is.] The woman is a master at keeping the shit-pot stirring, and it's all anyone can do but grab the popcorn bucket and watch.

On an unusually overcast May afternoon, Dandelion finds herself sitting at her desk, staring blankly at her computer screen, trying to ready herself to write. She feels *off* today. She woke up in a fog – no, it wasn't a hangover – and felt like she was moving in slow motion all morning. She is exhausted and even skipped her daily workout, which is totally unlike her. Instead, she opted for going back to bed after her girls had been picked up by the school bus. She is unable to focus on anything, doesn't have an appetite, and can't be bothered to respond to the slew of text messages pinging away annoyingly on her iPhone. Dandelion feels hollow.

Her helper, Imbali – which means flower in Zulu – nudges her gently and says in her Zimbabwean accent, "You okay? You don't look right. You sure you don't need anything?" Imbali looks regal in her purple dress with *shweshwe* fabric trim. She is a caring woman with a heart of gold and a pleasant bedside manner, who'd have made a hell of a nurse with all her patience and kindness. She is younger than Dandelion and left Harare for South Africa to make a better life for herself. What could Dandelion have to be so upset about?

She must think I'm crazy, thinks Dandelion. And without hesitating she replies, "No, I'm *fine*, Imbali, but thank you for checking on me," as if she has the answer cued. *You are pathetic*, she says to herself. Dandelion damn well knows she isn't fine; she's totally fucked up.

As the door closes behind Imbali, Dandelion sits frozen from the shock of realizing she can't keep up her charade any longer. Her internal fog lifts and she can clearly see again – she is done pretending to be perfect, fulfilled, and fine. She's exhausted by it all and just wants to feel real again.

She is tired of striving for perfection. Being perfect is a manufactured pipe dream created by photoshopped images of what some ad exec thinks a woman should be. No one is perfect. So why is she so hung up on achieving an unattainable status? She is so busy trying to be so damn perfect for the sake of others that she forgot who she really is inside.

She isn't fulfilled. Yes, she has a great life, but it isn't filling her internal cup of purpose. She doesn't want to be known as Oak's wife or Thistle and Wivi's mother. She aches to make a statement with her life, even if it only speaks within.

And lastly, she isn't *fine*. She is getting by, but she misses her old self. The Dandelion whose self-esteem isn't in the toilet and whose confidence isn't hiding. She no longer wants to shrug off those compliments and kudos but own them like she damn well deserves to.

Dandelion hits her breaking point. The happiness she felt has faded, and the raging fire once burning inside her has dwindled to a tiny flame. Dandelion's done her best to prevent her **#pilotlight** from being snuffed out, but she recognizes she's sputtering on the last fumes of gas to keep that flame aglow. She knows **#something** has finally made its last stand, and it's now up to her to figure out how to get her badassery back.

#MYTHEORY

Many badasses cope with confidence erosion, lack of purpose, and identity loss while living abroad. I wish it weren't so common, but this kind of crazy shit is legit life. It happened to me, and it can happen to anyone. It's normal, it's real, and it's nothing to be ashamed of. The good part is that when you recognize and accept it, it's totally possible to rein it in and take back control.

This kind of garbage silently creeps into an ASS's unsuspecting life and grows like a hibernating abscess. Most don't even realize it's happening. All the while, the ASS is doing her best to keep her chaos in check while trying to embrace her loss of control, feelings of resentment, and most definitely some denial. If you've never felt any of these things before, please spill the beans and share whatever witchcraft wards them off — because it's damn hard to rectify the situation once you go down the rabbit hole.

Only dead fish go with the flow

One of the main reasons I was propelled to write this book was to help ASSes realize they're not alone in their thinking. For a long time, I thought it was 'just me,' but it wasn't. As I began to identify what was causing my frustration, my mindset began to shift. I didn't yet know how to fix my problems, but I was at least aware of their existence. Before I could get to the real work of untangling my mess of emotions, I had to trudge up a mountain of bullshit to reach the summit. When I got there, I gave myself permission to embrace my truth.

Before I could get to that point, I had to work through a few critical points.

1. **I deserved all the feels**
   I could slap the old me for not allowing myself to lean into my emotions. I was feeling all sorts of things, and it was uncomfortable, so I pushed them out of sight into the back of my mind. I was too embarrassed to admit them out loud. Feelings about identity loss, lack of purpose, and confidence erosion are valid and deserve to be acknowledged. It's too easy to cover these feelings up with a phony *fine;* instead, we should accept and embrace our beautiful disasters. Life isn't perfect, and neither are we. So let's not do that anymore because we owe it to ourselves to be honest with our hearts.

2. **It was a long-ass journey to the breaking point**
   Friends, it took me nine years to figure out I had significant issues that needed to be worked on. Um, did you read that? NINE YEARS. This dumpster fire didn't just spontaneously combust. It was years and years of unattended smoldering trash that finally ignited. I didn't have time to realize *something* was missing because I was too busy buzzing around, trying to make sure everyone else's lives were picture perfect. Like I mentioned in *Chapter 2*, it was little fragments of self that eventually turned into a big missing piece. I didn't really notice a problem until it was too late. So if you see any signs of a deteriorating sense of identity, purpose, or confidence, don't hesitate to nip it in the bud because it's much easier to fix when there isn't as much muscle memory pulling you backward.

3. **I am so fucking worth it**
   For a long time, I confused self-worth with purpose. I felt like I lacked purpose – which turned out to be fulfillment – and that made me think I wasn't worth much. I couldn't have been more wrong. Worth doesn't equal purpose. Worth is when you value and love yourself for who you truly are – inside and out. It's not about what we do but who we are and what makes us unique. I was so caught up trying to prove my worth by creating a false purpose that I hadn't considered just how awesome I already was. And the *something* (fulfillment) I felt missing in my life was a puzzle worth solving. You, me, the ASS down the street – we're all worthy of our *something* because we deserve to be better than *fine*.

Come on baby, light my fire

I believe in things like serendipity and happenstance. I also believe knowledge is power – thanks to Sir Francis Bacon for saying it. So if they work in tandem, maybe they can create a better outcome. I didn't want to wake up feeling like my life had little purpose or feel like I was an imposter with eroded confidence or be played for a fool by a *friend* – but it all happened. The universe wanted it to occur, and so it did. I don't know why the universe does things – the good or the bad – it just does. But had I known to look for certain clues, I might have been able to change my bumpy path. Maybe it wouldn't have been as painful. I'll never know, but I hope my experience gives others some insight.

My experience is as unique as I am. Like no two snowflakes are identical, each ASS's process for uncovering their current state of self will never be the same. Mine was simply a moment of clarity among the ashes of friendship and at the mercy of craving more. Who knows, maybe you'll ugly cry yourself to sleep and awaken with a fire burning in your belly.

No matter how it unfolds, I hope you embrace it, feel it, own it, and hang on tight because you are ready for the ride of your life.

It's incredible how easily we forget who we really are inside and how hard it is to figure out where that badass disappeared to. So if we are given a chance, let's intensify our pilot light. Shelter it from the wind and help it grow into a mighty flame.

5

I meant to say it… just not out loud

#pilotlight

Sometimes the answer is right in front of you

Once Dandelion emerges from her bombshell moment of clarity, she becomes slightly obsessed with figuring out how to rectify her emotional cataclysm. She isn't sure where to start but figures the internet is as good a place as any.

"What do I search for?" she says to her laptop. She types in 'feeling unfulfilled' and a bunch of articles and blogs on the '10 reasons why you feel unfulfilled' populate the screen. She clicks through them one by one and notices many are written by coaches. She plows through numerous self-help books and listens to endless podcast episodes. She finds herself discussing the idea of fulfillment with everyone from her helper to her hairstylist. Sometimes you just have to tap the *#villagehelpers* for guidance, but no one's got anything revolutionary to suggest.

Even Thistle offers up advice. "Mom, have you tried YouTube? You can find anything on there."

"I'm not sure YouTube is my thing, sweetie. But thank you for the idea." Dandelion can't stand some of the stuff she sees on YouTube. What is it with people filming themselves playing video games or commentating while unwrapping toys? It's just weird.

"You should at least try, Mom. Isn't that what you always tell me?" Thistle says smartly. When her mother looks up at her, Thistle is wearing a smirk as she walks out of the room.

Dandelion's just been parented by her child. She'll search YouTube later, but she won't like it.

Still in search of what her next step should be, she asks Rosey for advice. She's levelheaded, doesn't waver, and always knows exactly what she wants. She's a badass.

"So, I'm curious," says Dandelion, trying not to make the conversation seem dire. "Have you ever felt a little like you've lost your way?" She's boiling water for a batch of pasta noodles and the steam is rising and fogging her glasses, which makes for good camouflage.

"Do you mean today or ever? Because I lose my way every day," says her friend.

"I mean like in life. Like, I don't know, maybe you need a push in the right direction." She's now cutting carrots, onions, and celery into cubes for Bolognese sauce.

"Oh." Rosey pauses to think for a moment. "Well, sure. I think we all go through that at some point. Before we moved here, I felt like my life was stuck in idle. That's when I decided to go back to work, tutoring part-time. I missed teaching and it got me out of the house."

"How'd you figure out what you needed?" inquires Dandelion, still chopping vegetables.

"Stumbled upon it really. It just came out one day when I was talking to my therapist."

Well, why didn't I think of that? Dandelion wonders silently.

With Rosey's story in mind, Dandelion seeks out a therapist. It isn't the first time she's toyed with the idea of seeing one. She's benefited from the experience a couple of times in the past and thinks it might be a good starting point.

She finds Gardenia on the Joburg expat group. She comes highly recommended and not a single know-it-all Nigella [you know the type] has made any comments about her. Plus, she speaks English. So there's no worry about lost in translation issues. Dandelion makes an appointment for next week.

Gardenia is a large-built woman with a heavy Afrikaans accent. Her voice is deeper than most South African women, and Dandelion finds it very calming. She likes Gardenia and believes they could've been friends under different circumstances. They are about the same age, have similar-aged kids, and she seems normal. This probably explains why Dandelion likes talking to her so much – Gardenia relates to Dandelion.

Over the weeks spent sitting on Gardenia's extremely comfortable sofa, which is perfectly placed in front of the window in her serenely decorated home office, Dandelion manages to feel less like she's the only one feeling off kilter. But she isn't feeling like she's on the cusp of any breakthroughs. Instead, she suspects she's just bitching about her First World life. Don't get her wrong, she's thoroughly enjoying (and deserves) one hour a week when she can unleash whatever's on her mind in a judgment-free zone. [Have you ever just bitched about whatever was on your mind to an empty room… no holding back at the absurdity of whatever might be coming out of your mouth? God, it feels good to just get all that shit off your chest.]

Dandelion ends up explaining to Gardenia that she doesn't believe her recent sessions are producing the outcome she is looking for.

In her uber Afrikaans-coated accent, Gardenia says, "Shame, Dandelion. There's no doubt you are in the weeds of some sort of midlife moment here, but to me, you seem to be very clear-headed right now. You seem to be searching for a resolution of some sort. What do you think you are searching for?"

Dandelion doesn't have a good answer to this question. She spends an hour each week in Gardenia's office unloading her feelings but doesn't leave with any inspiration on how to reignite the fire within her. "Maybe some guidance?"

"Hmmm. What kind of guidance? You need to be more specific," counters Gardenia.

"I don't really feel like I know what I'm doing with my life. Yes, I have a loving family, great friends, and a wonderful life. But *something* is missing. I need to figure out how to stop living on auto-pilot and start living with intention." Dandelion isn't quite sure where these words are coming from, but the floodgates open and she is like a plastic bag caught in the current. She keeps going. "I've talked to my family and friends back home in the US about feeling a bit lost, and they don't understand what I'm talking about. They think my life is one big vacation."

"Uh-huh."

"And my expat friends totally get what I'm talking about, but they don't exactly know what to do about it either. At least I'm not the only one feeling like I'm just treading water."

"Okay."

"And my husband, he's good and all, but this isn't something he gets. He's part of a corporate machine – I support the man who helps support the machine. Not complaining about that; we've experienced some incredible things because of our expat existence, but spare time is not exactly something Oak has on his hands. Plus, he's told me that I shouldn't worry about working because our life is a bit hectic and crazy, we move a lot, and he can't be relied on when it comes to his schedule or travel…" she yammers on. "I don't think he's being selfish; I just don't think he gets it."

Now that she can get a word in edgewise, Gardenia finally replies. "Well, I'm not sure you're technically looking for guidance because it sounds like you already know what you want, Dandelion. It seems like you're asking for permission to make it happen."

Perpetual PMS is not flattering on you

On another cloudless Johannesburg afternoon [FYI, Joburg afternoons are sunny like 95% of the time – it's a rough existence], Dandelion sits in the backyard with her legs dangling in the black-bottom pool, throwing a ball to her dog, and mindlessly scrolling through her phone for the umpteenth time. She notices a post about a free webinar being offered by Sunflower Seed, the coach she'd met at the GL conference earlier in the year, about how to create a globally mobile business. On a whim, the lost soul decides to enroll. She isn't sure what propels her to sign up. It's not like she wants to run her own business, but hey, what the hell does she seriously have to lose?

One evening, a week later, Dandelion logs in to the call and silently listens to the animated Sunflower explain, "With my help, we can work together to find your globally mobile business." [It wasn't quite so reminiscent of an infomercial – Sunflower is actually quite funny and a smart, engaging woman – but you get the gist.] D's camera is turned off and her microphone is muted. She feels like she's snooping as she watches and listens to the others behind her blacked-out screen. A checkerboard of faces covers the screen, and it reminds Dandelion of the *Brady Bunch* intro. After the presentation is over, people begin asking questions and the host does her best to answer the flurry of inquiries before the 45-minute session is over.

When the webinar finishes, Dandelion exits the call quietly and murmurs to herself, "I don't think that's for me. What kind of business could I really own?" She decides to let it go – at least she thinks she's let it go.

Weeks go by, but Dandelion keeps finding herself thinking about the information she heard during the session. Sunflower's presentation struck a nerve. During her presentation, she talked about developing a business idea but also emphasized things like living with purpose, finding joy, and being the best version of yourself. These are the exact things Dandelion is craving. The business part not so much, but purpose, joy, and a better self? Hell yeah, **#bringiton**.

But of course, in typical Dandelion fashion, she wavers. "It's just not the right time for me to make a commitment to something like that," she tells herself. Her head is getting in the way again, and she's trying to talk herself right out of taking the next step. [Oh, for fuck's sake, Dandelion.]

Meanwhile, if you observe Dandelion from afar, you probably think she totally has her chaos in order. And sometimes, when the stars are perfectly aligned, she has. But when those same stars have insomnia and can't sleep, she begins to experience short moments of raw internal madness.

When these moments materialize, she is amazing at covering them up with lame excuses and blames it all on having a bad day. But she starts to realize these episodes are becoming more and more frequent. Now, before you get all Judgy Juniper, let's clarify something – these episodes aren't anything most women haven't experienced. Dandelion might find herself losing her temper with her kids over something stupid like leaving the ketchup on the counter for the millionth time or has no patience for pretty much anything that doesn't go just as she expects – she is finding herself in a state of perpetual PMS. And it's not a good look. *Why can't anything go right for me today? What the hell is happening? Ugh, I'm just so angry. Woe is me. Blah. Blah. Blah.*

She's going through the motions of life, but nothing is changing *deep down*. She isn't finding joy in things she once loved. She's become guarded and is always questioning people's intentions. *Fuck you very much, Oleander.* And ultimately, her heart is aching for *something*.

Is a life coach like Sunflower Seed what she needs to help her determine what her *something* is? Could taking this leap of faith make her feel like her old self again? Maybe, but Dandelion's still having a hard time admitting she needs help to fix her derailed train wreck.

Fuck it

Dandelion's zodiac sign is Libra, and even though she doesn't really believe in astrological mumbo-jumbo, there's one thing that rings true when it comes to her celestial sign. She's completely indecisive. She'll research the perfect holiday destination for weeks, find a handful of perfect resorts that will appease the masses, get out the credit card ready to book it, but then fail to click the Pay Now button because she's afraid of making the wrong decision. It's ironic that the woman lives such an adventurous lifestyle.

After hemming and hawing about whether she should get in contact with Sunflower, she finally finds the *cajones* to reach out to her. "Fuck it," spouts Dandelion, and she uses her one fleeting moment of willpower to email Sunflower. [There's definitely a chance wine is involved.]

The act of contacting a life coach disturbs her. It makes her feel like a failure [um, no you're not] and ashamed for not being able to fix the situation on her own. Telling someone she's contacted a life coach would feel like full disclosure – like admitting she isn't in a good place. Which is true, but pride is a hard pill to swallow. She doesn't want to be viewed as a burned-out trailing spouse who can't hack it anymore.

For 10 years, expat life has been quietly chipping away at Dandelion's foundation, and it's now starting to crumble.

Dandelion's misconceptions about what life coaching really is will eventually be debunked, but this girl needs to learn the hard way.

Happy wife, happy life

On a cool Friday evening after Oak gets home from work, he and Dandelion are enjoying a drink on the back patio while the girls play in the garden. The candles are flickering on the table and Dandelion thinks this is a good time to mention the webinar and tell her husband about contacting Sunflower.

"I'm not sure why I reached out to her, I just feel like I need to do this," she says before raising her bottle of beer to her lips, a bit worried about what Oak's reaction is going to be. He rarely questions Dandelion's decisions and never gets on her case about expenditures, but she feels like this is different. Of all people, Oak's the one who's had a front row seat to Dandelion's life for the past 20 years. She knows he's aware of the sacrifices she's made over the past decade for their family and his career, but it's very unlikely he can understand what she's truly feeling inside.

Oak seems a bit surprised. "I've gotta be honest, honey, I don't really understand why you want to work with a coach." He pauses, takes a swig from his bottle, and continues. "But if you feel like you need to do something for yourself, you know I'll support you. It sounds like a big commitment." There's a lull in the conversation, then Oak continues. "So tell me about it."

For the next hour they sit at the table talking. Dandie explains how she'll meet with her coach twice a month and have self-study coursework. "I think it's going to be a lot like peeling an onion," she says. "I just want to be a better version of me and maybe find some passion along the way." She sits back in her chair and looks away from her husband.

"You know I think you're already pretty awesome, right?" He's looking straight at her as he speaks. "You don't have to try to prove anything to anyone, ever."

"Yes, I know. This isn't for others, it's for me." She's just admitted her truth – finally.

"Okay. So what's all this gonna cost?"

This is the part she's worried about – showing her husband the price tag. Dandelion hasn't made any financial investments in her life lately other than some Botox and a few Pilates classes, and she knows dropping thousands of dollars on a 'hopes and dreams' idea is risky. But in her heart of hearts, this is what she wants to do. "Well, it's not cheap," she starts and then goes on to explain the price structure in detail.

They sit in silence for a bit as they drain the rest of their drinks.

"I need another beer. Do you need a drink too?" asks Oak as he heads toward the bar fridge. "Sounds like there's a lot going on in that head of yours. I didn't realize you felt this way."

Dandelion fears the conversation's going to end without a proper finale. "So, what do you think? Do you think it's *#worthit*?" asks his wife.

"Dandie, I don't think the question is whether or not it's worth it, but whether or not you think you're worth it," Oak replies. "I know you're worth it. You should absolutely do it."

And now I'll do what's best for me

With her stomach churning, Dandelion waits for the Skype call with her new coach to connect. What's she going to say to this woman?

"Hi, I need to *#getalife*. Can you help me with that?" Dandelion murmurs to herself. She shakes her head in annoyance. It makes her ears bleed. "I can't believe I just said that out loud." [Ugh, it all sounds so pitiful, eh?]

"Hi, Dandelion! Oh my gosh, it's so good to see you! How are you? I'm so excited to work with you; it's going to be so much fun. You're the ideal candidate for this program and I can't wait to get started… I know you're going to kick this year's ass," proclaims Sunflower. "Oh, and you can call me Sunny."

Don't forget to breathe, Sunny.

Luckily, the person on the other end of the video call is a totally normal person who doesn't make you feel awkward. She has a great laugh, exudes confidence, and is funny to boot. The two women connect immediately over some silly thing, and this puts Dandelion at ease and allows her to really focus on what Sunflower is saying.

Sunny explains exactly what's going to happen during their sessions. "We'll work together to identify things you're struggling with, and I'll challenge you to dissect them to get to the root of the issue. It will take lots of hard work to overcome those challenges. But it's so worth it." This isn't going to be a bunch of online therapy sessions; it's going to be homework, hard work, and accountability – and plenty of self-reflection, lesson learning, lots of dreaming, and ultimately, action plan creation.

It all scares the hell out of Dandelion. *Well, damn. What the hell have I gotten myself into?* she thinks as Sunflower continues. Dandelion surely looks like a scared squirrel stuck frozen in the middle of oncoming traffic. She hopes she's at least blinking; she's pretty sure she isn't breathing.

"You look worried, Dandelion," says Sunny. "As we end this call, tell me what feels different now from when we started this session."

"Um, I don't really know," Dandelion replies, unconsciously wringing her hands. "I guess I'm feeling excited, but I'm just nervous. I have no idea why I'm really doing this; I just know *something* needs to change." Dandelion is overwhelmed.

"Exactly," exclaims Sunny. "Don't you worry. We've got this."

That last sentence changes things for Dandelion. "We've got this." She is no longer on this journey alone. As Dandelion ends the video chat, she feels as if the weight she's been carrying around like a Sherpa has lightened just a little. She has a big climb ahead of her but now feels like she has a partner to help get her to the top.

Seeking out Sunflower's help to untangle her madness is a turning point in Dandelion's life. She isn't sure why so many people – including herself – have been resistant or looked down on working with a life coach. It must be the name – Life Coach. Sounds sort of last resort-ish for anyone who doesn't know what the hell they're doing with their life. But Dandelion quickly discovers life coaching isn't that at all. It's for people who are ready to take control of their lives and challenge themselves to be the very best version of themselves.

Dandelion has become so famished for change that she is finally allowing herself to be completely vulnerable in the process of its creation. She is ready to tear down the walls holding her back from taking control of her fate. Her lack of confidence, absence of purpose, feelings of unfulfillment, and the distrust of her own gut are scheduled for demolition. It makes her feel naked – exposing all her imperfections. Dandelion is now on the path to rediscovering the woman who mysteriously went missing during the last 10 years. If she's going to turn her internal ***#pilotlight*** into a flamethrower again, she's going to have to start from ground zero. Totally stripped down and exposed. Dandelion feels ready to rebuild herself into a perfectly imperfect self-assured woman with goals, drive, and a full heart.

She never thought in a million years she'd acquire a life coach. But damn if it doesn't become one of her most stellar decisions ever.

#MYTHEORY

I'll let you in on a little secret: I didn't like asking for help. I know, shocking, right? But as I got older *and* wiser, I realized I couldn't do everything on my own, and, well, I didn't want to. Show me a law stating you must solely manage getting all your crap done by yourself. Besides, there were some things I just couldn't do alone, like fixing my confidence issues and figuring out what made the modern-day version of me tick. I needed some guidance on how to repair the chinks in my armor, and that's where getting a coach came into play.

If you can use an extra hand to figure things out and are able to acquire one, then do it, dammit. My friends, it takes a village, and these people are the villagers.

The best project you will ever work on is you

I admit it. It took some real self-coaxing for me to get a coach. I don't really know why; maybe it was my pride or an inflated ego. You should've heard the conversations going on between me, myself, and I. Ultimately, we all needed to get out of my way and trust the growth process (and my gut, but we'll get to that later). I got there eventually, but there were some important lessons along the way.

1. **Asking for help prevents failure**
   Duh. Let that sentence sink in a bit. If you got suddenly tied up and couldn't pick up your kids from school, you'd probably phone a friend to help you out. Right? Is that being weak or preventing failure? Failure would be your kids sitting on the curb after all the buses and other kids have been fetched by their parents and you getting a passive-aggressive phone call from the school secretary insinuating you need to get your act together. I've been there and done that. Calling in the cavalry is a way better option.

   Please never believe you're a failure if you think you need help of any kind. It drives me bat shit crazy when I hear ASSes, or anyone for that matter, say needing help is a sign of weakness. I mean, come on, people. What kind of garbage is that? That kind of thinking is only going to hinder us from growing. Reaching out for help is commendable and super fucking brave.

2. **Self-investment is worth every penny**
   I believe we need to take care of our wellbeing and personal development — it's not just for executives anymore — by investing in our future selves. We prepare for retirement that can be years away, but we somehow fail to finance what's happening right now. ASSes live busy and

complicated lives that need constant attention and come with added layers of expat stress. But at the first sign of an approaching market crash, we get scared and throw our personal priorities (AKA wants and needs) out the window for the greater good. Fuck that.

Yeah, sometimes these sacrifices are unavoidable, but we can't allow them to become habit. When we stop taking care of ourselves, we no longer live our lives at peak performance levels. Seeking out help increases our emotional balance for the short term and helps maintain it for the long term. So why wouldn't we put it at the top of our priority list?

3. **You don't know what you don't know**
   I had many misconceptions about what life coaching entailed. I didn't know it would help get to the root of what was causing my mental blocks. I thought it was just going to be a bunch of hippie-dippy kumbayas and self-praise – I didn't realize I was going to learn valuable life lessons and find the tools to keep me from going astray. I'm still by no means perfect, but I can now recognize when real issues start cropping up. I only wish I'd learned this stuff years earlier.

   I also didn't know coaches help people push through their bullshit – trust me, we've all got a load of it – and help their clients create a plan of attack to show the world just how big of an ASS kicker they really are. Life coaches are great at this. What do they have to lose when they call you out? Nada. They bust your butt when you make excuses for not giving it 100%. They're not your friend, nor are they emotionally tied to you. Coaches help make you find your full potential.

These lessons reshaped how I look at the importance of my personal wellbeing. The badass expat life is hard, and we need to take care of ourselves – plain and simple. As ASSes, we live in a constant state of transition and need to be pliable when it comes to the unknown forces continually shifting like invisible tectonic plates beneath our feet. If we take care of our wellbeing, we'll be better prepared for those strong, sudden shifts.

It takes a village *and* a vineyard

Remember the 'it takes a village' analogy? Well, it's totally true. Except as expats, our villages aren't the kind we might've been surrounded by while growing up. Our villages are diverse – a mishmash of cultures, languages, and identities – and they're woven tight by the experience of expat life. Only those who've lived as a foreigner will truly understand the intricacies of this type of village and the special kind of dependency and trust we place in them.

Villagers aren't just your friends and neighbors; they're people you seek out too. There are no limits as to what the villagers can do. The delivery guy at the local pizzeria who knows you by name – he's a village helper. The person who picks up your pooch for doggy daycare every Tuesday – they're a village helper. The girl down the street who watches your kids on Friday nights – she's a village helper. And, friend, I sure as hell know you have someone who touches up your roots because no one is brave enough to do that job on their own – you bet your finely coiffed tresses, they're a village helper too. Yes, I realize these are all First World village problems, but you know what I'm getting at. A life coach is just another kind of village helper.

By the way, do you know who heads up our villages? Us. We're the centermost point of the village – the command center, where decisions are made. And we have the power to make choices without having to ask permission. Yes, some choices warrant a discussion with other stakeholders, like our partner or spouse, but seeking out permission for happiness and fulfillment shouldn't be one of them. Supporting our village is a big job and it deserves a confident and content leader.

If you were talking to a friend who in a roundabout way was seeking permission to figure out their *something*, what advice would you give them? Would you say, "Oh, you'll get over it. You're just going through a phase," or would you say, "Friend, do what you need to do to make it right. I'll support you"? I'm putting my faith in humanity by saying this, but I'd sure as hell hope you'd respond with the latter. So take your own damn advice and do something about it.

6

That moment when you realize this *is* your circus and those *are* your monkeys

#truth

I'm pretty cool, but I cry a lot

Dandelion's first few sessions of coaching aren't exactly what she classifies as fun. In fact, if she must describe them, she'll call them a **#shitastrophy**. For about six weeks she's constantly queasy from the effects of the anxiety rotting away at her core. Every other week she logs in to a session with her uber-positive coach, hoping there'll be a breakthrough that'll miraculously cure her of this perpetual sour feeling.

"This feeling will subside," encourages her cheerleader. "I promise. It's all part of the process and totally normal to feel like crap at the beginning. The work you are doing is a four-phase process: (un)Covering Your ASS, ASS Kicking, Busting ASS, and BadASSery. You're in phase one, so hang in there."

Well, isn't that fucking wonderful, she thinks. *I'm so glad I'm paying to experience a perpetual hangover.*

Sunflower pushes Dandelion to examine herself in a different fashion. Each time Dandelion mentions a new issue, she's right there waiting with a piercing question. The questions are never invasive but dig deep.

"What causes you to feel this way?" Sunny might say with an inquiring tone. "Where do you think those thoughts come from?"

Embarrassed about the verbal diarrhea she spews – I'm not good enough, I feel like a fraud, I feel guilty, and her personal favorite, I'm just a mom – Dandie isn't prepared to deal with the emotional baggage, and it drains her. [Seriously, where the hell does this crap come from?] She can barely stand to look at the 'ugly cry' reflection glaring back at her during online sessions with a person she hardly knows. It's humiliating. Just because she's feeling a little confused about life doesn't give Dandie the right to bitch and moan about it. Or does it?

These first sessions produce insight into the deepest corners of her thoughts, and Dandie notices recurrent themes. Like peeling a giant reeking onion, layer by layer she uncovers a hidden clue to the origin of her shit storm. These feelings have unknowingly developed over years and years of expat living but are about to be exposed. Dandelion's about to learn her truth and begin the process of taking her power back.

Our worst enemy lives inside our head

"I'm so tired of pretending to be **#perfect**. If perfect is what they're looking for, I am seriously trying to impress the wrong people."

"Who are you trying to impress?" asks Sunflower.

"I don't know – the Judgy Juniper school moms and PTA Petunia and her arrangement of Chatty Cactuses for sure," says Dandelion, staring back at the screen and sounding annoyed.

"Why do you care what these women think?"

"I have no idea," she lies. "I just don't want them thinking they are better than me."

"So, you're trying to prove yourself?"

Dandie shrugs her shoulders in agreement. She knows exactly why she cares what those women think and what she's trying to prove. She wants to prove Oleander wrong.

"C'mon, Dandie. What are you not telling me?"

"Fine. But it's a long story." Dandelion proceeds to tell the entire Oleander story, in detail, to Sunny. "So now I don't trust myself like I used to," finishes Dandelion.

"Um, well, that's quite a tale. She sounds like a real piece of work." Sunny shakes her head. "How has this experience affected you?"

"Well, in the past, if I had a bad feeling about something or someone, I'd be able to sniff it out with a bit of women's **#intuition**. But now, I'm too damn scared of misreading the writing on the wall. I've been burned one too many times, and the last time this happened it took the wind out of my sails." An image of Oleander swims into her mind's eye, and Dandelion has to blink a few times to bat it away.

"Yeah, that can be hard. I understand what you are saying, but you've got to start listening to your intuition again," insists Sunny. "It's a powerful tool. It's your body's way of telling you if something is off. If you trust your gut, you ultimately trust yourself."

Dandelion can't even attempt to make eye contact with the shiny, smiley person in front of her. "I just feel like I can't make the right decisions anymore," she says. "There is something preventing me from being the person I used to be." A tear escapes her soggy eyes and she looks down at the keyboard to keep her advisor from seeing her weakness.

"Is there anything else you want to share with me today?"

Pandora's box is already open, so she might as well let out every single one of her dark secrets if she wants to fix this hot mess express. "I felt completely inadequate at the GL conference," admits Dandelion.

"What? You're kidding me. When I met you, I thought you were charming, interesting, and funny."

"I just didn't think I had anything to add to the conversation. It'd been years since I'd been to an event like that, and I felt extremely self-conscious."

"It sounds like your confidence has taken quite a hit. I'm very proud of you for admitting your **#truth**. I just wish you'd give yourself some **#grace**," remarks Sunflower. "You'll learn."

"Learn what?" asks Dandelion.

"To stop listening to your fearmongering inner critic and start listening to your gut." Miss Seed pauses for a moment. "We need to name that evil voice. How about Snapdragon?"

Dandie laughs. "Sounds like a proper mean girl to me."

"You're a resilient woman who is smart and kind. By putting Snapdragon in her place, you'll get back to being the badass you've always been. It'll be a game changer. Get ready to do some **#*damage*.**"

Fucking great.

Joining a cult sounds like a good idea – those people seem to have purpose

"Maybe I'm bored. According to my iPhone I've clearly got time on my hands. Yesterday it told me my Instagram usage is through the roof. I'm just wasting time scrolling through other people's lives."

"Alright," says Sunflower Seed, "we're going to try something. Don't get weirded out. Just close your eyes."

Dandie groans but cautiously closes her eyes. It makes her feel like she's on display – like a mannequin in a window. It's uncomfortable, but she listens to the instructions.

"Before we get started, I want you to clear your head." The voice pauses briefly before moving on to the next step. "Now, imagine collecting all the energy you waste each day doing things you don't feel are productive, and put them in a basket." Another pause. "This can include activities, things, even people."

In her swivel chair, Dandelion gently rocks from side to side collecting the things that zap her power. The addictive game on her phone that makes her nearly go blind from playing so much goes in the basket first, followed by the stretch of time she mindlessly scrolls through her phone, hopping from one app to the next. She plops all the bickering she endures from her girls into the basket and then scoops up the time she spends doing things for other people who don't seem appreciative of her time. Finally, she tosses in people who drain her with their drama and the unwanted aftermath of listening to it.

The voice begins again. "Have you collected everything?"

Dandelion responds with a whispered "yes" and continues to sit in darkness.

"I want you to try and pick the basket up," says the voice. "Is it heavy?"

Dandelion envisions herself trying to pick up the basket. It's heavier than she thinks it should be. "Yes."

"Do you feel how much extra weight you've been carrying around with you? Instead of letting each of these things take your power, you can release them and take it back to do things that make you light up with satisfaction." Sunny is smiling at Dandelion, but Dandelion has no idea. "Oh, you can open your eyes now."

She opens her eyes and squints to readjust to the light.

"What did you think of that exercise?"

"It was good. But I always feel silly when we do stuff like that."

"I know, but I don't care." Sunny laughs. "We aren't done yet."

"Oh, okay." Dandie readjusts herself in her chair. "What's next?"

"Now that you have that image of a basket full of energy-sucking sponges, what would you do if you could toss that basket off a cliff? What if all that stuff went away? What would you do with all that time and energy?"

"I have no idea."

"You can literally do anything you want – this is 100% about you."

"Anything?"

"Anything."

She takes a moment to think. It's harder than she thought it would be to dream of something only for her. "I'd buy an old house and restore it." Dandie's always wanted to take on a project like this but hasn't had a chance to while bouncing from country to country.

"That's amazing. Anything else?"

"I'd learn more about wine. Maybe take a photography class, learn to cook, or at least get some knife skills, go see the gorillas in Rwanda, hike Kilimanjaro. I'd definitely write more and worry less. I'd be more relaxed and less rigid." Dandelion's response takes her a bit off guard. *Where's all this been hiding?* "It sounds like a fairytale and a bit **#selfish**; I don't have a terrible life."

"It's not selfish," says Sunny. "And I'm sure you don't have a terrible life, but who's to say you can't have a more fulfilling one based on things you love or that pique your interest? You deserve to feel completely fulfilled just as much as anyone else." [Hmmm, sounds like someone is settling for a safe and common existence.]

"Yeah, I guess you're right, but I feel so *#powerless*. I can't rely on Oak to take over control of the house. He's not always dependable, because of work, and he travels a lot. And my girls still rely on me for pretty much everything. How am I supposed to just drop my obligations to them and do something for myself?" [Sounds like a lot of *#excuses*.]

"Um, Dandelion, that's what I'm here to help you with! You are totally capable of figuring this out, and with a little help from me, you aren't going to feel powerless anymore. You're so worthy. You are going to feel like you are full of purpose when I'm done with you."

Dandelion catches a glimpse of herself on the big iMac screen. Her arms are crossed and her lips are pursed in a frustrated side pucker. She doesn't look comfortable, and, well, she doesn't feel comfortable either. She really wants to buy into all the great things the woman whose advice she's paying for is saying. She does, she really does, but the skeptic inside her is yelling *#talktothehand* and stops her from believing what sounds too good to be true.

I sure as hell hope you know what you're doing, Sunflower.

Nobody knows who I really am, including me

While getting ready for her next coaching session – lipstick and blown-out hair ready – Dandelion tries to recall what it felt like to wake up and prep herself to take on the world each morning. You know, adulting before the responsibilities of marriage, kids, dogs, and globe-trotting the world transformed her life into a myriad of athleisure clothes and dirty hair ponytails instead of smart business casualwear and coiffed tresses.

It never used to feel like a chore to be confident and focused, and Dandie wonders where that badass faded to as she slips a hair straightener through her blonde locks. Not wanting Sunny to get the best of her today, she finishes her face with a swish of pink gloss across her lips and hopes she can get through this session without messing up her mascara.

"Tell me some of the things you enjoy doing in your spare time," sunny bloody Sunflower begins their next weekly session. "What makes you feel good inside?" *Why is this woman always so damn perky?*

"Um, well, I like to work out. Does that count?" She feels her resolve weakening the moment the words tumble out of her mouth and senses her shoulders beginning to slump in her freshly-ironed shirt.

"Maybe. Is working out a passion or something you do because it's good for your mind and body?"

"It just makes me feel good – period." Dandelion enjoys going to the gym because it's a place where she feels connected and sure of herself. "I might not be the best athlete in there, but I feel satisfied every time I leave in a sweaty state."

"Okay, yes – tell me more about these kinds of things. I want to know what fuels your soul."

"I like watching my kids ride horses."

"That's what your *kids* enjoy doing in their spare time. Right now, we're talking about *you*."

"Right." Dandelion wants to crawl under a rock. She can't name one more thing she loves doing. *What the actual fuck?* There's a long pause before she continues. "Well, I like to take ballet classes. I take a class once a week with a group of teachers who are training for certifications. But I only do it when I have time. It's not a priority or anything."

"Is there a reason it's not a priority for you?"

"My kids are my priority. They're getting older and need me less in some ways and more in others. I'm trying to keep my role in their lives **#relevant**. I didn't feel this way 10 years ago. When Thistle was a baby and I still had a career, I would lean on Oak more to allow me to find time to do the things I wanted to do for myself because I still had obligations outside of the home and felt like I deserved them."

From the expression on her face, it's clear Sunflower doesn't like what her client has just said. "And?"

"I guess, over time, a lot has changed – I don't contribute the way I used to all those years ago. I started staying home full time, then we moved overseas, his career took off, and I became the board of directors of our household—"

"I'm sorry to interrupt you, but your worth is not your work. But we'll talk about that another time because you're very deserving of stuff – no matter what it is – even if you don't work outside of the home. [Give her hell, Sunny.] I feel like there was a but coming. But?"

"But I feel an enormous amount of **#*guilt*** when I dream about me. I don't even know what I'd do. I don't really know who I am anymore. Fuck. That's a scary thought." As she finishes her statement, Dandelion realizes that even though her words are negative, her back is straight, her eyes are dry, and her voice is unshaken. She's going to get through this.

"I bet it is, but you're definitely not the first person to feel this way. One day you will know exactly who you are. You'll look back on this moment and think, 'Who was that person?' This process is going to be so amazing for you."

God, I hope you're right, thinks Dandelion, *because that shit sounds downright pitiful*.

Is 'done' an emotion? Because I feel that in my soul.

Happy the first eight weeks of her transformation are over, Dandelion starts feeling much more comfortable with the coaching process and no longer feels constantly nauseated by her situation. If there's a single thing that's come from her overly-emotional word vomit, it's speaking and accepting her **#*tru*t**h. [Thank the fucking gods for signs of progress!] This ASS is aware things aren't going to change overnight, but she's determined to get her badassery status back.

For the past decade, she's been bottling up the little things that have bothered her about her **#*happy*** life. With outside guidance and a lot of grit, Dandie has exposed the realities she'd been afraid to admit. Years and years of loneliness, resentment, guilt, boredom, dissatisfaction, and sadness finally built up enough pressure to break the seal and allow an enormous rush of emotions to bubble out like a shaken bottle of champagne. It's incredible what a little push can do.

Dandelion decides to break her silence about her secret life coach while at dinner with her friends one evening. "Oh my god, you guys. It's validated the fuck out of all the things I thought I wasn't allowed to feel. I thought I was just being overly dramatic. Who knew it was okay to feel your feelings?" She sips her wine. "It hasn't been fun, but I've learned so much about myself in such a short time."

The group of friends is supportive of Dandelion's decision to find someone to help her untangle her knotted emotions because that's what friends do – they support you. "That's great, Dandelion" and "I'm so happy for you" are the kinds of responses she receives from her all-female support group. She should never have doubted they'd say any different. But that's what internalizing Snapdragon's harassment does; it makes Dandie believe her bogus chin-wagging is gospel.

For years, Snapdragon's been telling Dandelion to stop making such a big god damn deal about feeling a bit lonely or a little bored every time she's moved. The bully tells her to stop dwelling on the fact that she isn't using her brain like when she had a paying job, and that instead of complaining, she should feel appreciative and lucky to be able to stay home with her children. [YES, she is lucky and appreciative, but it doesn't mean she isn't allowed to still want to use her brain for more than singing 'The Wheels On The Bus.'] The only one telling Dandelion to simmer down is Snapdragon, and it's time to put that loudmouth in her place.

The relief of having off-loaded the weight of her emotional baggage into a holding area gives Dandelion a chance to soak in her achievement and ready herself for the next stage of the process. She accepts her truth at face value and is keenly aware of the massive amount of work ahead of her. She imagines it will be a bit like unpacking an enormous suitcase full of hoarded goodies after an extended trip back home, but it's a piece of luggage she has zero intention of ever refilling again. She's ready to unpack this one for good and takes that as a sign of confidence seeping back into her life.

Dandelion puts her faith in Sunflower and prays the human ball of energy on the screen has a method to her madness. What she's been discovering about herself hasn't always been easy to accept, but she understands it's a crucial part of her development.

"Dandelion, you did it," announces Sunflower as they begin their next session.

With a confused look on her face, Dandelion replies, "Did what? I'm not following."

"You did it! You made it to phase two. Welcome to the ASS Kicking phase."

"Sweet. What does it mean exactly?" responds the clueless mentee.

"It means you are ready to start the next stage of learning to change your life for the better. I won't lie – it's not a walk in the park. None of the work we'll do is going to be easy. But as you know, it will be worth it."

"Super." Dandelion's ready, but as with most things, she's got a little anxiety because it's uncharted territory.

"I've put together a plan for us to follow during this next phase to help you harness your power and get your badassery back." Sunflower claps her hands and fist pumps the air.

Individually these lessons are important, but grouped together they're a one-way ticket to reclaiming the status Dandelion lost somewhere along the way.

#MYTHEORY

We've all got something we don't like about ourselves, and no matter how hard we try, sometimes that shitty little thing we don't like gets the best of us. For me, it's the stretchmarks around my belly button, along with not being able to do jumping jacks or skip rope without having to wear an adult diaper. They're both little reminders of just how much this petite 5'2" woman who didn't have great birthing hips enjoyed being pregnant. Believe me, I realize I'm lucky on many fronts, and the side effects of pregnancy and giving birth could've been much worse. But it didn't mean my feelings weren't valid. These things happened and I didn't like it – I found the stretchmarks unattractive, and, well, peeing yourself in public is humiliating.

For a while I listened to the bully in my head sling insults, telling me bikinis were off-limits and that I should stop doing exercises that made me feel like my pelvic floor was going to fall out of my body. I'd examine my scarred navel or feel my dignity running down my leg – it was too late; the damage had been done. Over the years, I've flushed loads of money down the drain trying expensive creams and voodoo oils to make the scars vanish, but shockingly, they didn't work. And you'd regularly see me sneaking out of exercise classes to relieve myself of three drops of urine in case the trainer planned to make high knees part of the next workout.

I have no idea what prompted me to stop worrying about those minor issues. I guess I'd just had enough of the self-imposed limitations my inner critic had been placing on me (though I had no idea what an inner critic was at the time). I was lucky to be the mom of two feisty girls who push my buttons like I'm a video game controller, and these flaws were proof I'd given them life. Owning these weaknesses became a testament to love, strength, and honor between me and my girls. Overstretching my skin to make more room for them to grow and having my bladder pay the price to push their heads out of my vagina is no fricking weakness – I'd say that's pretty badass if you ask me.

In this case, hushing the narrow-minded heckler from voicing her opinion happened completely by chance, but I've gotta say it did feel incredible to throw that bikini back on. The peeing myself thing will always be a bit humiliating, but at least I now know I'm not the only one doing it: another woman admitted to me that it happened to her too. Solidarity, sister.

The first 40 years of childhood are always the hardest

There were a few things I learned early on in my coaching process that helped create the relationship I have with myself today. I emotionally stripped down till I was naked in the messiness of my feelings, which in case you're wondering, is a super fucking uncomfortable place to exist. I felt extremely vulnerable because I no longer had the emotional shelter of my double-agent inner critic telling me to stand down.

1. **Weird is a side effect of awesome**
   Validation is a funny thing. Do we need it from outside sources? Absolutely not. But as a recovering validation seeker, it's pretty sweet when it falls unprovoked and organically in my lap. There's nothing like hearing someone say, "OMG. I feel that way too," or, "I thought I was the only one." It doesn't make the journey easier, but it does make it a little more bearable knowing other people can relate to your current crisis.

   I didn't work with a coach for the validation — it just happened to be a byproduct of the work I did. Maybe I could've tried doing all of this on my own, but I doubt I'd have been as successful as I was. Working with a coach streamlined the process by keeping me on target and walking me through the tough stuff when all I wanted to do was run to the finish line. She also helped me accept that my emotions, thoughts, and behaviors were valid, which helped motivate me to keep moving forward.

2. **Don't blame me; my inner critic is an asshole**
   Before working with a coach, I had no idea the voice inside my head had a catchy name, let alone the muscle to produce such distortion. I learned my inner critic was nothing but a liar and all-around mean girl. She literally

made shit up about me, my friends, my enemies, my family — my entire existence. Figuring out my inner critic could be shushed jumpstarted the process of rescuing my confidence and taking back my power. My inner critic was doing a great job of holding both of those precious things hostage. I'm not saying she still doesn't try knocking on my door; I'm just much quicker at slamming the door in her face. Sounds simple, right? Well, it is and it isn't. It takes a lot of practice — hell, I'm still practicing every single day.

I don't blame myself for letting her get the best of me. It's probably because adulting is hard and I let my guard down, but more likely, over time I was conditioned to think the things I said to myself were anything other than true. And when one part of my existence got a bit weak, the stronger and more aggressive part stepped in and acted as if it was going to throw it a life preserver and instead sunk it faster than the Titanic. Having awareness that she, my inner critic, exists makes it much easier to control her crazy talk.

3. **Liquid courage: getting drunk and saying everything you ever wanted to say**
   Speaking one's truth is an act of courage. Many people are afraid to voice their stories because they fear people won't believe them, or they worry people will judge them, or they'll judge themselves — or all the above. In a world where I'm sometimes a bit spineless, I take comfort in knowing I'm now capable of being honest with myself and can accept my story without judgment. I don't always like the truth, but hey, at least I know it's not a lie.

   Being able to own your truth — exposing it and embracing it — is powerful stuff and was a total game changer for me. I'm not saying it was a super fun and easy process, but it certainly opened my eyes to understanding what was causing the emotional rollercoaster I couldn't seem to get off. Labeling the things that frustrated me was liberating, and accepting them was an act of self-love.

By learning the significance of empathy, honesty, and love for the current version of who I was (and for future versions too), I began shifting my life's trajectory. These little nuggets of hard-earned badassery helped me rebuild a solid foundation of self-acceptance and propelled me into the next phase of the coaching process, where I continued to learn more and more about all the shit I packed away for all those years and tried to forget about, just like the random box of crap that never gets unpacked each time I move.

I wish everything was as easy as getting fat

If there's one person who should wholly support you, it's yourself. Far too often we minimize how we feel, breeze past our killer accomplishments, and hide behind the walls we erect to keep us from being an army of badasses. And here's the thing; there are so many ASSes scattered around the world feeling the same kind of emotions and having the same kinds of thoughts. We aren't alone in this fight. Living abroad can shoot a plethora of emotional punches at an ASS. The damage inflicted can vary from a fat lip (making language mistakes) to getting knocked out cold (losing your identity). If we keep taking big punches, we'll tire of fighting back and eventually get knocked out.

That's where my coaching experience stepped in and taught me how to take punches, slip past some, and how to throw my own. Unlike a psychologist, who analyzes a patient's psyche, coaches coax the client into identifying what is hindering them from moving forward in life. Digging through all the dirt allows the client to get to the root of the issue.

I continually remind myself of the way I felt during those first couple of months. It was simultaneously scary, sad, and surprising, but it helped me begin redefining the new me. Being able to rise above the bullshit is powerful — whether it's your own or someone else's. This is the kind of badassery dreams are made of; it's not impossible, but you just might need to get naked first.

7

I told you so...
Sincerely,
Your Intuition

#trustyourgut

If something feels off, it is

"Name your intuition and send me a text letting me know what you've chosen," reads Dandelion. It's a text from Sunny – another homework assignment.

Sitting on the corner of her comfy brown sectional sofa that's traveled more miles than many passports, Dandelion ponders names. Unlike Snapdragon, who is sneaky and persuasive, her intuition has, or at least did have, a positive aura – capable and protective but blunt enough to say "I told you so." She knows Dandelion's deepest, darkest secrets and is capable of blackmailing her confidant to Timbuktu and back, but she'd never turn her back on Dandie. An image of a floating pink lotus flower drifts into her mind. It seems like a fitting name. She grabs her phone, types LOTUS, and presses send.

Full of honesty and truth, Lotus is feeling a bit let down by Dandelion lately. Over the past decade, Dandelion's become great at second-guessing Lotus' innate capabilities.

Rosey's description of Dandelion had been a spot-on assessment, and it haunts her. "You're always trying to find the good in people. And I love that, but sometimes you try so hard searching for the good that you miss the bad." It's obvious from Rosey's statement that Dandelion doesn't know when to trust her gut about first impressions.

This doesn't just apply to people but to physical things and commitments too. This pisses Lotus off. Big time.

If Dandelion goes shopping for a new dress, she'll stare at herself in the mirror hemming and hawing over whether the fit is right or if it makes her look like she's wearing a potato sack. *It's okay,* she'll think to herself. *I definitely don't love it, but it'll do.* [Way to **#trustyourgut**, Dandelion.] Settling for something she can absolutely live without is just another way of telling her intuition to sit down and shut up. That dress will inevitably hang in the closet collecting dust with its price tag dangling to remind her of her poor fashion choice. Each time Dandelion goes through her closet she'll feel too guilty to throw the damn thing out.

Or, when PTA Petunia or one of her Chatty Cactuses asks if Dandelion wants to help plan the school fundraiser, she'll reluctantly say yes even though Lotus is whispering, "That's a hard-fucking no, Dandelion," in her ear. Our little blondie is always reacting quickly and making on the spot decisions about things she really doesn't want to do because she doesn't want to disappoint anyone. Why is it okay for Dandelion to fulfill other people's needs and not her own?

It's no wonder Lotus went on sabbatical. What will it take for Dandelion to learn that her intuition is the most truthful friend she's ever going to have in her life?

Sometimes I want to go back in time and punch myself in the face

"What's on your mind today, Dandelion?" pipes the computer.

It's a sweaty Joburg summer afternoon. Storm clouds are rolling in from the south, and from the sight of the dark sky brewing in the distance, Dandelion knows there's going to be a magnificent light show. The air is thick and heavy. She's feeling depleted – hot, tired, and unmotivated for her session with Sunflower. She isn't sure how she's going to get through the next hour without looking like she'd rather be floating on a flamingo raft in her pool or napping with the aircon on full blast.

"I must admit, I'm not feeling very focused today," reveals Dandelion.

"Well, you don't have to admit anything. Your energy says it all." Sunflower continues to nudge Dandelion as if she's poking a hibernating bear. "Why don't you tell me what's going on?" [Way to rein in that **#RBF**, Dandelion.]

That's the funny thing. Dandelion really doesn't know what's going on with her; she just kind of doesn't feel like playing today. Lately, she's been feeling disengaged, disinterested, and more reclusive than normal.

"Honestly? Not a hell of a lot," admits Dandelion. "I'm just feeling blah. My head feels clouded."

"Help me understand what you are feeling," pushes Sunflower.

"Okay. Let me think." She pauses a moment. "I've been noticing that I'm having a hard time making simple decisions." Dandelion has occasionally seen this issue pop up over the last few years, but it's become more apparent recently.

"An example would be helpful."

"It's embarrassing because my example is lame." She hides her face in her hands.

"Get over yourself, Dandelion," says her slightly annoyed coach. "Lay it on me."

"I want to buy a new sofa." The beaten-up brown sectional pops into her head. "I've wanted to buy a new sofa for six months, and I've gone to the store a dozen times. I've picked the same style twelve times. I've even chosen the same fabric but have never walked out of the store actually ordering it." She pictures the pile of color swatches lying on the console table in her living room. All of them are the same distressed gray leather. Dandelion clearly knows what she wants, but she keeps hesitating and second-guessing herself. "It's like I don't trust myself to make the right choice. I mean, I'm choosing the color of a fucking couch, not the wire that will or won't diffuse a bomb."

"Um. Duh. Did you just hear yourself?" Sunflower is holding her hands out with her palms up like she's pointing out something **#obvious**. "You don't trust yourself or your intuition whatsoever. What did you say you were going to call your intuition? Lotus? You're not listening to what she's telling you, and it's been punching you in the face the entire time."

"It's such a dumb example, the couch thing."

"No. It's not. It's not do or die, but it's *so* real. Do you even see what you're doing to your gut each time you walk out of the store without buying the couch? You're allowing Snapdragon to overrule Lotus, telling Lotus she doesn't know what the hell she's talking about. You and Lotus *both* agreed on the same thing twelve times. You're letting the bully get the best of you." Sunflower is staring at her with a look that says 'you know I'm right.'

There's an uncomfortable silence, but Dandelion knows Sunflower is on the mark.

"Over the next two weeks I want you to do some homework. First, I want you to still your mind and get back into your body. I'll send you the exercise via email so you can read through it before you give it a go. I know you don't like the hippie-dippie stuff, but you're gonna do this." From all the complaining Dandelion's done about previous attempts at getting her touchy-feely with her mind, Sunflower knows her client will hate the exercise. "Next, I want you to get a notebook and pen and start journaling. And last, I want you to recognize how your body feels before you answer any question regarding commitment. Try to gauge how you feel – does the idea excite you or do you feel automatic dread? Really think about it and note the energy your body is giving off." Sunflower's wearing a stern expression and Dandelion feels like she's trying to hammer her point home. "When you and Lotus get on the same page again, I believe you'll feel like nothing can stop you."

Meditation: because we could all use a little sit down and shut up

A few days after her session with Sunflower, Dandelion's still putting off the homework assignments she's been sent. Knowing procrastination is going to get her nowhere, she opens up her laptop and clicks on the document link for the meditation exercise.

This kind of assignment is hard for Dandelion because getting all hocus pocus and kumbaya makes her feel awkward. Obviously, getting in touch with her inner self isn't one of her strong suits, which probably means she needs to do it more than ever. Carefully reading through the assignment and trying to keep her eyes from rolling into the back of her head, Dandelion attempts to keep an open mind. She finds a quiet space where she can relax, a place where she can lie down, close her eyes, and try to feel every part of her body – from the tips of her toes to the hairs on her head – without touching them. Opening her mind to feel things from the inside out is the first stop on an apology tour for Lotus.

Reluctantly, she lies down on the cool tiles of her bathroom floor, places a rolled-up bath towel under her head, reaches her hands out wide, and tries to relax. After lying there for a few minutes trying to get comfortable, she finally succumbs to the exercise but not before getting up to pee and checking her phone one last time.

"Just lie the fuck down and do this," she grumbles to herself.

Finally comfortable on the floor, she starts trying to 'feel' the tips of her toes. Slowly, Dandelion begins moving up through her feet – metatarsal to tarsal – rounds her heels, and makes her way up to her ankles. Keeping her breathing steady and her mind on the prize, she needs to bat away Snapdragon and her sniggering laughter from a dark corner of her mind. "Oh, would you just shut up," snaps Dandelion. The sniggers end immediately, and Snapdragon recedes.

Inching her way up her legs, through the bigger muscles of her body, she converges on her lower back, where it feels tight. She makes a mental note to book an appointment to get that worked out. As she reaches her belly, Dandelion senses an electrical burst of warmth and welcome, and she imagines threads of blue and purple light emitting from her midsection like a plasma lamp. *Oh, hello, Lotus.*

She continues up her chest and makes her way from the ends of her fingers to her shoulders and the base of her neck, where Dandelion notices an enormous amount of tension. Snapdragon is there, silently hiding in the dark corner of her being like a predator waiting for an opportunity to catch its vulnerable prey. She continues through her throat and into her head, where she points out each tooth, her ears, nose, eyes, and finally her brain. Her brain is churning away and knows it's time for Dandelion to let it rest. As she finishes the exercise, she senses the split ends of her highlighted blonde locks, makes a mental note to schedule a haircut, and takes one more moment to feel her entire body as one. Slowly, she opens her eyes and realizes how relaxed she feels. It's like she's cleared a new path for herself.

Having nothing else on her agenda for the afternoon, Dandie decides to close her eyes again and lies on the floor for an extra minute. Floating somewhere between total relaxation and a catnap, she doesn't hear her housekeeper enter the bedroom. Imbali's wearing headphones – listening to music on her phone – and doesn't spot Dandelion lying on the floor of the en suite. As she turns the corner to enter the bathroom, Imbali drops her bucket and mop and screams, suddenly waking a startled Dandelion.

"Huh?" mutters a half-asleep Dandelion.

"*Eish*, man! Are you okay? What are you doing laying on the floor? Do you need help?" stammers the out of breath woman who looks like she might have just had the biggest scare of her life. "I thought you were dead."

"Oh, uh, I'm okay!" Dandelion jumps up and grabs the towel from the floor. "I was just working on a meditation exercise." She places the towel back in the basket and smiles at Imbali. "I didn't mean to frighten you."

"Well next time can you please meditate on the bed and not the floor like a dead person?"

Bad vibes don't go with my outfit

Recognizing her reaction to things isn't as hard as meditating because people have no clue she's doing it. It's designed to appraise her initial thoughts about decisions. Later, this barometer of sorts will be the basis of creating boundaries, but right now, it's a simple tool to get back into sync with Lotus and keep tabs on Snapdragon.

These body responses aren't always blinking neon signs warning her about suspicious people and dubious situations. They can be as subtle as a meh feeling when she's being offered a free glass of bubbles that's too sweet for her liking (especially when the calories are definitely not worth it). It's amazing how receptive she is to the silent messages being sent from within. She hasn't completely stopped making decisions based on how other people feel yet, but with each opportunity, Dandelion does notice when she's feeling excited or frustrated.

"*Hola*, Dandelion! *Cómo estás?*" waves Begonia as they're both heading toward the cart corral in the center of the shopping mall parking lot. "I have not seen you in a long time. You want to have a coffee with me?" Begonia is a Columbian mom she knows from school. The woman literally has her finger on the pulse of everything and is the local repository for all things gossip related. She's also a yoga instructor. Not just yoga – hot yoga. You know, the kind where the room is a large sauna, and you attempt to keep your feet from slipping as sweat drips from every orifice of your body. To Dandelion it is nothing but *#gross* and her version of a personal hell.

Do you want to have a coffee? That's a good question. It's only 10:30 a.m., which is still an acceptable time to drink coffee, but she's already had three, including the two americanos she drained after boxing class. She has groceries to buy, errands to run, and the dogs still need to be walked, all before her doctor's appointment that afternoon. Dandelion also knows the spandex-clad Begonia is going to press her about why she hasn't taken her up on her repeated offer for a free trial hot yoga class. And lastly, Dandelion's got the sneaking suspicion that Begonia will try to get info on why she and Oleander are no longer chummy. Dandelion knows Oleander frequents her yoga studio and would want in on the latest scuttlebutt.

Dandelion really doesn't feel like she has the extra time today, but Begonia's been reaching out to her over the past couple of months and she'd feel guilty blowing her off again.

To make matters worse, Snapdragon butts in. "Now, you don't want to disappoint Begonia, do you?"

And so going against her true feelings, Dandelion says sullenly, "Hey, Begonia. Sure. But just a quick one because I have a long to-do list today. Alright?" [Wah, wah, waaahhhh.]

Begonia doesn't seem to notice the tone of her voice, but Dandelion sure as hell does. She instantly felt a jab in the gut from Lotus as the words fell out of her mouth. For the next 45 minutes, Dandelion sits there dodging questions and feeling resentful about her continuing inability to listen to Lotus.

"I told you so," is all Lotus silently mumbles to herself for the rest of the afternoon as Snapdragon watches Dandelion hurry around like a chicken with her head cut off and is five minutes late for her doctor's appointment.

In the deepest, darkest corners of Dandelion's psyche, Lotus sits chewing her lips, waiting for the next time she'll be called upon to use her powers. "Surely, she'll listen to me eventually," she hopes. "She has no idea what we'll be capable of when we finally join forces."

Your gut knows what's up – trust that bitch

As a young girl, Dandelion always kept a journal. Filling hardbound notebooks with her most private thoughts was always an enjoyable thing for her. She can still clearly remember the time she found her much older brother reading her preteen thoughts while lying on her plaid-clad twin bed and laughing uncontrollably. He mocked her and made her feel like an absolute loser. At that moment, she decided never to journal again.

For years Dandie has preserved her thoughts by tucking them away inside her head like a secret Filofax vault. She knows she may have lost some memories by doing this but has always been fearful of someone discovering her innermost thoughts again and what they would think.

As an aspiring writer and an adult with a better sense of judging where to hide things, Dandelion begins journaling again. Her head feels as jam-packed as an overflowing file cabinet in desperate need of a purge to make space for new thoughts. She buys herself a beautiful pink leatherbound journal and makes a promise to write in it often. Every few days, she sits quietly and allows her pen to scribble her unique hybrid handwriting – half cursive/half printing – and unloads a data dump of her mind. She uses Sunflower's idea of being in touch with how she is feeling during moments of decision and focuses her journaling on what her body is telling her.

After a while she begins to spot recurring subjects – how a specific person makes her feel uneasy or how a kind of situation makes her feel completely carefree. Dandelion writes how some days it's harder to let Lotus take the reins but knows her hesitation is due to not yet being completely comfortable with letting her heart control her head. Her mind's eye isn't wearing a veil anymore, and Dandelion has a clearer view of her decision-making process, which is really beginning to piss Snapdragon off.

"*I'm much more comfortable with the choices coming to me from within, and it's becoming easier to let go of the hesitation,*" she writes. "*I'm letting my gut guide me instead of my fearmongering mind.*" Take that, Snapdragon.

Lotus feels as if Dandelion's finally given her the thirst-quenching drink of water she needs to keep going. This simple nod of trust breathes new life into her. With Dandelion no longer making Lotus feel like the forgotten sidekick who never gave up on her friend, the pair can now move forward as a powerful team.

#MYTHEORY

The Persian poet Rumi wrote: "There is a voice that doesn't use words. Listen." He wrote this in the 13th century, way before the saying 'hustle harder' was a state of mind. Even back then, Rumi knew that our intuition is a silent guide leading us down the path of life. I'm assuming life was simpler albeit much harder back then. Remember, Genghis Khan was running around trying to kill and conquer anything in his path, and there wasn't a constant need for instant gratification and the adrenaline high of how many likes your post on Instagram just received. Come to think of it, 1995 was a hell of a lot simpler than today too. God, I miss the 90s.

Rumi was smart. He was saying that we each have a special power inside of us and that we need to quiet our minds to hear it. If we can stop our head from bullying our heart, we can become more aware of the cues our body naturally produces. It's like giving the gift of listening to yourself.

Listen to your body – it's smarter than you are

I'm multi-faceted when it comes to clearing my head and touching base with my intuition. Routines are important to me, but I also like having options to change things up on occasion. Maybe it keeps me on my toes, maybe I'm just lazy – it really doesn't matter, as long as I commit to doing it.

1. **Inhale the good shit, exhale the bullshit**
   I'm terrible at meditating for long periods of time. My mind wanders and I can't help but scratch the itch on my back when I'm supposed to be sitting still in silence. Knowing I struggle with this area of my life, I've discovered a different way to meditate – I do common daily tasks without added outside noise and distraction. I walk my dogs without listening to a book or podcast, I cook without the TV on, and I shower without listening to music. While I'm doing this, I'll take deep breaths to brush away the cobwebs and help me focus on the task at hand, feeling each step of the process. I don't always do these things without noise, but when I feel like I'm not in sync with my gut, I find it helps me to be more reflective of how I'm feeling in the moment.

2. **If you see me talking to myself, I'm having a staff meeting**
   I don't know about you, but I talk to myself a lot. Like, all the time. Don't look at me like I'm some sort of nutter because I'm sure many of you reading this book do it too. I feel like getting the words out of my head helps me better understand what I'm feeling. I work through all sorts of things, from family issues to how I'm going to tackle a busy week ahead. I like capturing this mind madness, and occasionally I'll review it to see how far I have come in the growth process.

Journaling
As often as I can, I give myself five to ten minutes to unburden my brain to get all the random thoughts and ideas out of my head and express how I'm feeling. Early mornings and right before bed work best for me, but the timing is different for everyone. I just start writing and see where it takes me.

Audio Notes
When I don't have time to sit down and write longhand, I'll hit record on my phone and talk it out, just like I would with a friend. These little blurbs of candid conversation sometimes catch some brilliant wisdom and great advice. It's like chatting with my intuition.

Having one-sided conversations gives me time to reflect on how my body compass is feeling and reacting. If it feels light and open when I think through an issue, it's signaling to me that I'm on the right path, even when that path is bumpy and full of potholes. But if my instinct shuts down and I feel guarded, there's a good chance the solution I've come up with is a shit sandwich and should be tossed out the window.

3. **Nobody listens to me – the yellow traffic light**
   Another quick and dirty method I like to use to get in touch with my intuition is the traffic light strategy. It's an easy way to gauge my internal barometer and look for silent nudges from my intuition. Just like a traffic light, there are three colors of initial reactions. Reading the green and red signals is easy; it's the yellow ones that are a bit tricky.
   - green = yes
   - yellow = maybe
   - red = no

   When I get a green light feeling, I instantly want to shout "Hells yeah!" I'm certain and without a doubt happy or excited by the idea that I've just heard and feel nothing but joy. My whole being feels open to the opportunity. If I sense a red light, I slam on the brakes with a "Hard no!" I get an immediate feeling of dread and ick, and the idea sends warning sirens off from all corners of my body.

The yellow light technically means caution, but many of us tend to be in a rush and try to beat the light. If I hurry into a decision and don't really give my gut a genuine chance to process, I might not make the right decision. For small or rather insignificant decisions, I stop and then breathe three times. Doing this lets me pause long enough to give myself a chance to get feedback from my gut. For bigger decisions, the phrase 'let me sleep on it' comes to mind. Maybe that's because I tend to have more clarity when I wake up in the morning – unless I can't sleep, which also tells me something. This signal is my intuition asking me to gather more info to make a better decision. If I jump the gun and blurt out yes or no, I might end up regretting it later.

Your intuition is literally a private instant message from your body – do not let your head turn it into a group chat

Relearning to trust your gut can be a long ride on the struggle bus to redemption. When you've been pushing aside your internal wisdom and second-guessing what you knew was probably right for as long as I did, no wonder my intuition threw her hands up in frustration and went on a permanent vacay. I truly never thought my intuition could get so out of whack.

I completely derailed my body compass. My inner critic was super aggressive and acted like an invisible dictator in my head. I believed anything and everything she babbled on about to be true. Just like the mean girls in my high school cafeteria, she talked down to me and made me feel like I was nothing but a dorky loser who had no idea how to climb the social ladder. That's what bullies do and it's a bunch of crap. Her overpowering voice led me to doubt my intuition, which led me to develop a deep desire to prove myself. Why? I think it was because I wanted to feel like I was powerful, but I'm not sure, and that pisses me off.

Had I just listened to my gut when I knew deep down things didn't feel right, it would have kept me out of some pretty shitty situations. This lack of listening didn't happen like flipping a switch; it was learned over time. Years and years of doubt and stupidity. I could have saved myself a lot of wasted energy, frustration, and sadness. Hindsight is 20/20, but it's a good thing I'm not dwelling on the past; there's no sense in beating myself up for the mistakes I've already made. I can only move forward with the knowledge I've gained and urge myself to quiet my mind and listen to the fire in my belly — not the loudmouth in my head.

8

My brain has too many tabs open, and I can't figure out where the music is coming from

#overwhelm

Friendship is finding people who are your kind of crazy

"What's up, *chicas*?" Dahlia asks cheerily as she tosses her gray braided hobo bag onto the rattan lounge chair next to where Dandelion is lying quietly on the pool deck. Dandelion is cradling a **#skinnybitch** – a vodka soda with lime – and looks as if she's taking a nap.

"Not much," says Dandelion, "just living the dream. You?" She doesn't even open her eyes.

"Good god, I needed to get the hell out of my house tonight. The boys and Spruce were at each other's throats, and I just couldn't tolerate their bitching anymore. I have no idea what they're going to eat for dinner, but there's a full fridge and a stocked pantry. No one will go hungry." She grabs Dandelion's glass and swallows the rest down. "You need another anyway." She shakes the ice cubes in the glass and walks away.

Just then, Rosey steps onto the patio holding an overflowing platter full of cheese, meat, crackers, olives, and fresh fruit. "Feast your eyes on this," she says as she sets it down on an enormous granite countertop, then twirls around behind the bar to find a bottle of bubbles to pop open and start the evening. Rosey's patio is a suburban oasis with large palm trees and perfectly placed lighting. "Where's Mags? She said she'd be here by now."

"Hi! I'm right here." There's a popping sound as Mags enters the patio. Instinctively, she heads straight for the bubbles. "I couldn't escape Maple. He has a science project due next week and it's currently living on my dining table. I've been working on it with him all afternoon," she says, rolling her eyes. The ponytailed friend has speckles of green glitter on her face, which triggers a feeling of anxiety in Dandelion. She imagines a sparkling sea of emerald on the floor. *Glitter is never a good idea.*

Dandelion gets up from the lounge chair and makes her way over to the bar to join her friends. She scans the sun-kissed faces of the women she calls her anchors, knowing how lucky she is to have found the three of them. This tight foursome can solve the world's problems with a cheeseboard and a good Chenin Blanc, create frosted masterpieces for their kids' birthdays, and come up with an excuse not to cook when you don't feel like cooking – which is often.

This small posse of friends is ever accepting and loving, and Dandelion never feels alone in the world knowing she has them to lean on. She doesn't worry about what they'll think of her if she shows up in tattered jeans, without makeup, and empty-handed. Their specialty is accepting each other for the perfectly imperfect women they are and loving each other despite their **#flawsomeness**.

So much to do, so little desire to do it

As the friends take their places at the bar for their ladies' night, Dandelion notices the vibe is somber. This group and the word somber don't particularly go together, so she knows something is off. There's a tired energy hovering around them. Not a 'I didn't get enough sleep last night' kind of tired, more of a 'I'm worn out from adulting' kind of tired.

"Friends, what the hell happened to us?" asks Dandelion. "We used to be so energetic."

"I feel like I haven't slept in weeks," spouts Rosey as she pours more fizz into Dahlia's flute. "Attending university classes six time zones ahead is killing me – I can barely get through the day without taking a power nap. I'm like a three-year-old."

"I don't feel tired in a sleepless way, though I'm sure I could use some extra hours of shut-eye," Dandelion chips in. "I guess I feel weather-beaten like a favorite pair of jeans that are barely held together by their seams. They've been worn so many times the threads are thin and about to break. With one false move my butt cheeks are going to completely fall out."

"Yeah, I know what you mean," agrees Dahlia. "I'm constantly chasing my tail. Sometimes I feel like I'm on a hamster wheel." She cuts a slice of cheese and puts it on a cracker. "I'm juggling way too much, but I don't feel like I can drop anything." She pops the cheese-topped cracker in her mouth.

"I wonder if all women feel like this," says Mags. "I mean, I'm sure they do. Life in general isn't easy, but then our expat lives aren't run of the mill. Living thousands of miles from the support of family and friends adds an extra level of difficulty." As global nomads, they all know this is true.

Each one of the women sitting at the bar has lived a global life for more than a decade. They've left fulfilling careers, given birth in places where they couldn't speak the language, packed up and moved their families to new unknowns multiple times, and done it all in their stride. If there ever was a private club of badass expat women, these four were ideal candidates for membership.

The four women sit in comfortable silence contemplating tonight's conversation. Dahlia's blonde-highlighted hair glimmers in the candlelight across from Dandelion and matches the shade of the champagne glowing in their glasses.

"Do you guys ever feel like you could crawl out of your skin and just walk away from it all?" says Dandelion eventually. "I know that sounds terrible, and I don't mean a 'never come back' kind of walk away. But sometimes I just get so fed up and feel like I need to lock myself in the bathroom, have a small mental breakdown, and give myself some privacy to figure things out." Dandelion realizes she's just vomited *#TMI* all over the bar.

By this time, she's been working with Sunny for a while and is much more capable of putting her feelings into words and accepting them – but it doesn't mean she's conquered all the things that are bringing her down yet, nor is she aware of how to overcome them.

"Yep. Almost every day," answers Rosey.

Oh, thank god, thinks Dandelion.

"It just hits me out of nowhere," continues Rosey. "Kids are playing loudly, food needs preparing, I'm being asked the thousandth question of the day, and I'm worried about the assignment I've just submitted to Uni." Rosey gets it. "I realize I haven't spoken to my parents in weeks because the time zone is so difficult to manage, Elm keeps asking me if we've been reimbursed for the health insurance claims that I never submitted, and I have to get new passport photos taken for the entire family because we need to renew our passports." She really gets it. Dandelion's in *#ingoodcompany*.

"Same shit happens to me too," Mags says, topping up everyone's drinks. "It's normal."

"Is it normal, though?" asks Dahlia. "I rarely see Spruce lose his mind." She takes a sip of her drink. "That seems to be my job, and I'm pretty damn good at it. I've had lots of practice."

The friends laugh but they know it's not a laughing matter.

Panic attacks are my cardio

A text message pops up on the computer screen. "Ready when you are." It's Sunflower letting Dandelion know she's ready to start their session.

"Oh, crap," curses Dandelion. "I thought our session was at 11 a.m." Dandelion looks down at her watch to see it blink 11:01 a.m. "Dammit." She quickly slaps the keys to let Sunflower know she needs a few minutes. Still in her gym clothes and with her hair looking completely unkempt, Dandie has been trying to make reservations for an upcoming weekend trip to Cape Town with Oak. "Shit." She smooths her hair, pinches her cheeks to add color, and pushes the call button on her computer screen.

"There you are," smiles the red-lipped wonder. "Everything okay?"

Dandelion is self-conscious about her appearance, so she needs to pull herself together quickly. "Oh, yeah. I just lost track of time." She smooths her hair again. It wasn't a lie. "Don't mind the way I look. I didn't get a chance to shower yet."

"I couldn't care less about how you look. I'm more interested in what's happening with you. Tell me how things are going."

Dandelion still hates being prompted and doesn't enjoy jumping into tough topics. Why can't there just be a magic switch that propels her into the future, where things are moving along smoothly? *Because this is real life and not a make-believe world created by a five-year-old*, she reminds herself.

"Things are alright," she begins. "I've been working hard at listening to my gut. I think putting in the extra effort has been helpful, and I'm starting to see some changes there. Though I'd obviously like it to go faster." She can't tell if she's making this sound better than it actually is since she's never happy enough with her progress.

"That's great news. It's always a positive sign when you begin recognizing changes within yourself."

"I am, but I'm also noticing something that isn't so great." The words spill from her mouth before she has time to stop them from falling out. "I'm losing my shit a lot lately. It's like my temper has the shortest fuse."

Sunflower looks back at her as if she is telepathically urging her client to keep talking.

"You know when your husband comes home and tells you that you're moving to another country, and you get that feeling like there's so much shit to do and you don't exactly know where to start?" asks Dandelion.

"Oh yeah. Totally," chuckles Sunflower. As an expat who's moved several times in recent years, Sunflower knows exactly the feeling Dandelion is describing.

"It's not that at all. I can handle that kind of big stress with some sense of control because I know it will eventually work itself out. The move will happen, our family will get settled, and life will go on. It's hard work to get to the new destination, but so much of it is out of your control that you've just got to roll with the punches. But with this... it's different."

"Say more," presses Sunny.

"It's the little things that seem to be piling up." Dandelion stops for a moment to collect her thoughts. "I feel like it's all on me."

"What's all on you?"

"Everything. I don't have a typical job," says Dandelion, using air quotes on the word typical. "I work from the moment I wake up to the second I rest my head at night. Yes, I know that I am a stay-at-home mom, that I'm a trailing spouse [bite your tongue, Dandelion] – I mean ASS. And that I gave up my career for our family to take on this exotic adventure called life. But fuck. I'm so over it right now."

"How do you feel when these emotions bubble over?"

"I just get this feeling like I want to crawl out of my skin. Everything starts to seem like a tremendous hurdle to overcome, and I can't manage to do the simplest task without getting frustrated." Dandelion hates to admit it, but she feels like life is too much sometimes. Not like she wants to give up on it, but more like she's in a constant state of floundering.

"Ahhh. Okay. Yup."

"Yup, what?" retorts Dandelion.

"It's called **#overwhelm**."

"Super. So what does it take to get underwhelmed?"

"Well, a little reflection to start. I know how much you love it when I tell you to do this kind of thing." Sunflower gives Dandelion a teasing look. "I think you've got to start by identifying what makes you feel overwhelmed. What triggers this response from you? And you need to see if there are any patterns. For example, does it happen at the same time of day? If so, we can put some practices in place to help prevent you from having a downward spiral." She pauses for a moment. "When is the last time you felt like you were going to crawl out of your skin?"

Dandelion doesn't say anything.

"Don't overthink it."

"Tuesday night when I was cooking dinner," blurts Dandelion.

"Before that?"

"Monday morning before the school bus."

"And before that?"

"Sunday night before bedtime."

"Are you noticing anything?"

"Yes. When there's a hard stop – like a bus pick up or a bedtime – I become unhinged."

Dandelion's answers are forming a clear pattern: she gets flustered when she's pressed for time. When she feels pressed for time, she tries to accomplish more than what is possible. When she tries to accomplish more than what is possible, she starts making mistakes and ends up a pissy wreck.

"But there are other times I also feel completely buried," says Dandelion. "Like I don't know where to start and no one else is involved. I just can't figure out how to get started." Dandelion looks frustrated; Snapdragon feels like she's on top of the world.

Sunflower smiles. "Same but different. It's still a state of being overwhelmed. We'll work on that too."

momster (n.) – a mom with zero patience who turns into a terrifying beast

"It's time for dinner, girls," Dandelion calls, but no one comes to the table. She calls again. No answer. She calls again. Silence. She stomps into their bedrooms and makes sure they hear her loud and clear. They look at her like she's a raging lunatic.

After finally getting Thistle and Wivi seated at the table, their stressed-out mom tries to see how their days have played out. "What happened at school today, girls?"

"Nothing," says the oldest.

"I dunno," answers the one who clearly hasn't listened to the question.

Oak isn't home from work yet to help carry the conversation, and she quickly runs out of things to say because her day's been rather uneventful too. The three of them continue to eat their dinner in silence.

After the girls finish eating and skitter out of sight, a long-beaked African hadeda swoops into the garden, squawking like a pterodactyl. This provokes the dogs to run in circles and bark uncontrollably at the bird, who perches on the roof and starts taunting them from above.

"Thistle! Wivi!" hollers their mother. "Come on down here and clean up your dinner plates. This isn't a restaurant with busboys and dishwashers."

"In a minute."

"I'm busy."

"Now, please," calls their mother, who just wants to get the kitchen cleaned up so she can rest.

There is no response from the girls.

"Girls, I'm losing my patience."

The mobile phone on the counter begins to rattle and ding like a pinball machine reaching a high score. She accidentally spills a glass of water. Upstairs the girls start bickering. Her sense of touch becomes electric, her ears begin to ring, and she feels like she's baking in an oven. Then she snaps. "Enough! I can't take anymore."

Normally, she does take more, a lot more. And Oak usually arrives home to find World War III in full swing. He'll tiptoe around his wife like he's attempting to traverse a minefield, doing his best to duck and cover his way through eating the dinner left for him on the stove and making his way upstairs to change into his pajamas before taking his post on the couch while Dandelion continues with the siege. And she thinks, *How can he just sit and watch me lose my shit every night?*

Met with the repeated resistance of "no" or "later," she typically surrenders to the dishes on the table because there's no more fight left in her. Inevitably, she also packs the snacks, fills the water bottles, and dismisses showers for another night.

Too exhausted to relax and unwind after the girls are finally asleep, she finds herself climbing the stairs for bed feeling bitter and resentful that no one can do anything for themselves. Not that she gives them the chance to do it for themselves. It's easier for her to do it herself because there's less arguing and less room for error – and less time for Dandelion to do what she really wants to do, which is sit her butt on the couch and watch Netflix.

But tonight, it's different. Instead of Dandelion going on a rampage like a female version of Rambo, the drained badass reminds herself of the advice Sunny gave her during their last session and takes control of the situation before it goes completely off the rails.

She hears Sunny's voice in her head: "When you feel like you're starting to get overwhelmed, take a moment to stop and breathe. Remove yourself from the situation and give yourself a chance to regain your composure so that you don't have an adult temper tantrum."

With the night-time chaos surrounding her, Dandelion walks into the garage, closes the door, and stands in the quiet darkness. She no longer hears the dogs barking or the girls bickering; she can't see the mess on the table or the empty snack containers on the counter waiting to be filled. Allowing herself time to calm her mind and body resets her mood and gives her the energy to get on with the night without losing her shit once again. It doesn't mean she's excited about the work she knows she'll end up doing, but at least she knows she's making progress.

"You've gotta walk before you can run," Lotus reminds her.

Some days I amaze myself. Others, I can't find the phone I'm holding in my hand.

"Where do I even start?" laments Dandelion. She's staring at her computer screen. "I have so much to do, and I don't know how I'm going to get it all done." She picks up one of the writing assignments Hawthorn is waiting on. "I've got to get to work."

A second later, the phone rings. It's one of the Cactuses asking if Dandelion's got the information she volunteered to pull together for the school fundraiser. *Shit!* thinks Dandelion, *I totally forgot.* Before hanging up, she assures the Cactus she'll get her the info ASAP.

She clicks on the email icon on her computer screen and opens an inbox full of unanswered emails. Some of them are important and others are just reminders, but it's a lot to look at and she really needs to clean it up before something else important gets missed.

Lately, Dandie's felt like she's been fighting to get out of a pit of quicksand. There's an overwhelming number of things needing to be done, but she can't get started with any of them. These long-term projects are quickly growing into festering problems because of excuses and procrastination. The daily routine isn't affected, so the only one noticing there's an issue right now is her.

Having always been a fan of list making, Dandelion was surprised when her coach told her that something as simple as making a list is a good way of overcoming bouts of overwhelm. Dandie scours her desk for the list she made the other day. Finding it under a pile of doctor bills needing to be submitted to the insurance company, Dandelion reviews the numbered list. It takes her a while because there are 27 items scribbled on it.

Snapdragon immediately cackles, "There's no way you can tick everything off this list today." Which is probably true given the list looked like Santa's Christmas list.

"Yes," Dandelion agrees. "Giving up is easier than getting started, but some of these are really important. So go to hell." Forcing herself to face the things she's been avoiding is enough motivation to shut Snapdragon up. "Besides, I'm not listening to you." Her inner critic looks like she's been burned, but Dandelion doesn't notice. She scans the list again. "Okay. What must get done today?" She highlights the five most important items on the list in pink, and the next five in blue.

The entire afternoon is spent working at her desk. One task after another is chipped away from the list. Within a few hours she's surprised by the amount of work she's done. Grabbing the list again, she scratches the last highlighted task off with a big black mark. Dandie feels accomplished for the first time in ages and is inspired to keep going. She prepares for the next day by highlighting another set of tasks in pink and blue.

Writing deadlines are no longer going to be avoided till the eleventh hour where she ends up worrying if she's produced the best work possible. The bills aren't going to pile up risking late fees – it only happened a couple of times, but they were avoidable mistakes she's embarrassed about and a secret she keeps from Oak. An aloof scatterbrain isn't who she wants to be, and it isn't who she really is in the first place.

Rethinking and simplifying things makes Dandie realize she's been setting herself up for failure. There will always be items on the list waiting to be checked off. Tasking herself with what's achievable helps build back the confidence she lost and keeps her from feeling like a failure when her laundry list of chores can't be done in a day.

This little flower is ready to get off her rollercoaster and start cruising a little more. But damn, it's hard to keep working on all the different things she's trying to change within herself. Dandelion knows it's worth it – that she's worth it – but her drive occasionally wavers from the fatigue of working so hard.

When she's almost ready to give in to weakness and Snapdragon's wicked ways, Lotus chimes in to shut it down. "Nothing worth having comes easy, Dandelion. Trust me."

#MYTHEORY

I now know I get easily overwhelmed, so I no longer take calm moments for granted. I try to be mindful of when life offers up stiller waters – like when my kids are happy and not stressing out over friends or school or some other teenage drama. There's a good chance it's only going to last for a hot minute, so I enjoy the shit out of it. Another example is when I feel comfortable in my host country – when I can confidently walk into an establishment and accomplish whatever I'm doing while barely making a fool of myself. These moments don't last forever, so when they do occur, I absorb the good juju that radiates from them to keep me going later.

Unless you hit the euphoria jackpot, these low-stress life breaks probably won't happen simultaneously with other aspects of your life. I might be struggling with my kids but have a strong relationship with my husband, or my family ties might be awesome, but my friendships are strained. I've had to learn to recognize the good stuff intermingled with the bad because life is never going to be perfect. If it is for you – well, you might be reading the wrong book.

Being an adult is like folding a fitted sheet

I'm the kind of person who likes order. I like my spice cabinet to be arranged with all the labels facing forward, I like my closet to look like a rainbow, and I like my desk clean and tidy. Yep, I'm a weirdo. I accept my odd quirks as *Claire Flair*.

So when my life gets shaken up like a snow globe in the hands of an uncontrollable toddler, it does my head in and turns me into a raging lunatic. Before I can move forward again, I must hit the reset button or at the very least press pause to let the snow fall back to the bottom of the glass ball. My body gives me a signal when I'm getting overwhelmed – I'm kinda like a volcano. Pressure slowly builds from deep inside, and I feel my emotions bubbling up like hot magma. Sometimes a blast of ash will warn me about the looming eruption of exploding lava. Except my flare-up usually contains expletives like something from an X-rated version of *Mommie Dearest*.

I despise the frenzied feeling of overwhelm and helplessness that sometimes takes over my body. Good thing I kicked helplessness to the curb because now I know how to calm the Mount Claire volcano before it erupts. Not always, but a hell of a lot more than I used to. Through the coaching process, I figured out I was rigid. Hell, I still am. I like things my way. Doesn't everyone? But in my world, if things didn't go exactly how I envisioned them, it was a failure. I couldn't have been more wrong. By being consumed with making everything go to plan, I didn't leave any room for error, which was completely unfair and unrealistic.

1. **I prep for my sanity**
   Mornings are my downfall; I'm always racing around trying to do more than humanly possible. Knowing this, I prioritize a few extra minutes at the start of each day to set myself up for success — have a coffee, brush my teeth, put on a bra, and check my calendar. If I don't, I'll be focused on everyone else's needs and I'll be trying to take care of my own at the same time. It sounds so basic but being able to solely focus my attention keeps me from getting frustrated in the morning. By identifying what triggers my overwhelm, with a little preparation I can avoid these issues.

2. **I tap out before I get pinned**
   Like any good tag team, sometimes you've gotta let your partner get in the ring. ASSes and their partners both work their tails off, but my reality is both mentally and physically draining. From AM to PM, I'm *doing*. It can be wearing, and sometimes it catches up with me — that's when I ask for help. Yes, I'm a capable and independent woman, but if I'm not making a situation better, I have no shame in looking at my husband and saying, "You're in." So many ASSes don't ask their partners for help because they think, *it's my job*, or, *they work so hard all day*. I hate to break it to you, but so do you. There's nothing wrong with them having some skin in the game to give us an occasional break.

3. **I plan my escape**
   When I lived in Mexico, I'd often get overwhelmed at birthday parties. I couldn't keep up with the conversations among the Mexican moms at my daughter's school. They knew Spanish wasn't my native language and tried to slow down, but they'd forget, and I'd be confused again in no time. To keep going — to persevere like a badass — I'd excuse myself from the situation just long enough to regain my composure, clear my head, and steady my heartbeat. These little mind breaks have worked for me in numerous

situations – from screaming toddlers to patronizing PTA moms. It's better to walk away for a few minutes than to let yourself get frazzled and say something you don't mean.

4. **I get distracted intentionally**
   There's nothing like feeling overwhelmed when you are in a situation you can't escape. I was once the president of an international women's club and I'd often have to speak at meetings. I'd get nervous anticipating having to take the mic to speak. I figured out a way to inconspicuously disrupt my mind by pressing my nails into the palm of my hand – the sensation was enough to keep me from thinking about being nervous. Massaging between my index finger and thumb is another good one. I also try to take some deep breaths because they're easy to hide too. Doing this gives me a private space in public where I can get my head clear.

5. **I tick it off my list**
   I love lists and make a hell of a good one. I find them super helpful in organizing myself when I feel like I'm drowning from the daily grind. If you feel like your list is too daunting, break it into chunks. I highlight the top five must-complete tasks. If I do them all – great – and because I'm a badass, maybe I'll try to knock out a couple more. But if I don't complete the top five, no sweat – I take the remainder of today's list and leave what didn't get done for tomorrow. Do yourself a favor: don't set yourself up for failure.

6. **I measure my own success**
   It dawned on me that success can be measured in many ways; it just depends on how you look at it. I consider my children boarding the bus and arriving on time for school a success – even if they don't brush their teeth. Showing up to Teacher Appreciation Day empty-handed isn't worth losing sleep over. And skipping my language lesson this week isn't

going to derail my entire academic career. Important things are still happening – my kids are getting to school on time, I'm showing up to help even though I forgot to make a quiche, and bailing on a language lesson might be what this badass needs to get through the day. They may not be triumphs worthy of history books, but they sure as hell answer the question "Did anyone die?" with a very loud NO. Will anyone die from my kid not brushing their teeth? No. But maybe someone makes fun of their stinky breath and tomorrow morning they'll brush their teeth before school. It's doubtful, but one can dream.

Try not to murder anyone today

They say 'cooler heads prevail' and they're exactly right. If I can bring myself back from the brink of losing it, there's no doubt that I'm an unstoppable force to be reckoned with. All that flying off the handle and acting like a mighty lunatic gets me nowhere fast. So it's a good thing I figured out how to stop myself before I go ballistic. But just because I have a giant bag of tricks now doesn't mean I'm perfect – I'm far from it. I still lose it, just not as often.

Looking back, I hadn't noticed the blow my confidence took each time a wave of overwhelm knocked me down. Years of these emotional tsunamis enabled my inner critic to chime in with negative self-talk, and it had to stop. I might not be Wonder Woman, but I'm sure as hell worthy of not having to listen to that kind of bullshit every time I fall.

Change is a lesson in resilience. Learning to be more pliable didn't come naturally and made me uncomfortable – which was a good thing. As I became more acquainted with these new behaviors, my mind started to adapt, and my confidence grew stronger. Learning to deal with my overwhelm and making those cray-cray episodes a thing of the past is very rewarding and led me to a better place — as a wife, a mom, a friend, and a badass. I deserved better and so do you.

9

You can't make everyone happy – you are not tequila

#boundaries

A lack of boundaries invites a lack of respect

"What's for dinner?" asks Wivi as she clambers into the car with her arms full of backpacks and riding gear.

"Hello to you too," Dandelion says to her sweaty and tired-looking daughter. "I made chicken satay with peanut sauce and noodles."

"Ugh. Chicken? I hate chicken," whines her other child, who is now tossing her stuff into the trunk. "We always have chicken."

"Actually, Thistle, sometimes we have beef or lamb." Dandelion's trying to lighten the mood in the car, but her attempts at comedy are obviously bombing.

"I'm not eating chicken sa-sa-sa," stumbles the little one from the back seat.

"It's satay, Wivi. And yeah, neither am I. No one wants peanut chicken. Can't we just go out?" barks the other one.

Dandelion twists round to look at her daughters. *You two have got to be fucking kidding me.* "Nope. We aren't going out. I've already cooked it."

"But I don't want peanut chicken!" snaps Wivi. This time her words have a little more attitude.

"Wivi, I've already told you. We. Are. Having. Chicken. Satay. You've never even had it before, how can you say you don't like it?"

Dandelion can feel her blood pressure starting to rise. She presses her nails into the palm of her hand; she's not feeling overwhelmed but is still getting worked up.

"Why do we always have to eat what *you* want?" interrupts Thistle. "We never get to choose what we eat."

"You can choose what you eat when you are adults and have your own money." Dandelion is getting really irritated now. She takes a few deep breaths to steady herself.

"You can't make me eat it!"

She doesn't know who screamed it, but this sentence sends her over the edge.

"That's enough out of you. I'm your mother, and you will eat what I tell you to eat! I don't want to hear another word. Stop being so **#ungrateful**," shouts Dandelion. She is disgusted with their behavior. Her children hadn't even said a goddam hello before she was being berated for not making them happy enough.

The girls are crying now. They're exhausted from a long day at school and overheated from riding in the hot sun all afternoon. Their dusty faces are beet red, and tears are streaking down their dirty cheeks.

Dandelion feels like shit. She pulls into the garage and opens the trunk. As she's standing with the girls unloading the car, Dandelion caves by waving a white flag of **#defeat**. "If you don't want to eat the satay, I'll make you pasta. Would you like that?"

"No meat," declares the blonde militia in unison.

"No meat. Just sauce."

If you don't like being a doormat, then get off the floor

Sunflower sits listening to Dandelion recount the satay story.

"I know this wasn't one of my best parenting moments," Dandelion confesses, "but I'm struggling to figure out how to keep from repeating this kind of scenario daily. I'm being walked all over like a **#doormat**. I feel like we're headed for our own episode of *Dr. Phil*."

This wasn't the first time the girls had led a successful *coup d'état* against their mother, nor would it be the last, but Dandelion doesn't know how to engage in the battle. She's been worn down by the dynamic duo over the years and doesn't have the fight or the patience in her anymore. She gives up quickly to keep the peace, and her daughters are really used to getting their way.

"Oh, and let's not forget how guilty I feel after I yell at them. The **#momguilt** is relentless."

No matter what the outcome, Dandelion always felt sick with guilt. How could she holler at her kids that way? What kind of mother was she? How could she let them get away with that kind of behavior? How will they ever learn to respect their elders? She shoots Scud missiles at herself from every angle. At this rate, she's never going to get parenting right. *But who really does?*

"Dandelion, I think I'm hearing you say you're lacking **#boundaries**. Tell me where I'm wrong," says Sunflower.

Dandelion shrugs in agreement. "I guess."

"Okay, so I suggest we come up with strategies to prevent you from getting trampled by your mini stampede. The first strategy we'll work on is asking yourself what you'll no longer accept, and then you'll stop accepting it."

"So, like, I no longer accept being treated like crap by the little monsters I brought into the world?" chuckles Dandelion.

"Well, yeah. So make a list and then start pushing back on those behaviors. You're going to change the way you allow others to treat you. You deserve to be treated with respect. We all do."

The next day Dandie sits at her desk and pens a short yet concise list of things she's no longer going to tolerate from other people. She writes: *Being disrespected, Being taken advantage of or for granted, Being responsible for other people's problems.* She looks at the list for a long time thinking how hard it's going to be to set these boundaries and stand strong when they are tested. "This should be fun," she says to the list as she tacks it to her bulletin board.

Stop asking why they keep doing it and start asking why you keep allowing it

"Mom, why didn't you wash my shirt?" bellows Thistle from down the hall.

"Um, let me think, because you didn't ask me to. I'm not fucking Nostradamus," Dandelion mutters under her breath as she puts the milk back in the fridge. "Do you need it washed today?" She places a bowl of cereal on the counter for her prickly tween and pulls out a barstool to sit down.

"No. It's too late. I needed it for today," sneers Thistle as she takes her seat at the breakfast counter. Her tone is harsh and completely uncalled for. "I told you yesterday."

"Actually, you didn't," says Dandelion defending herself. "I'm pretty good about making sure you have what you need when you need it – if I'm given a heads up. I would've made sure your shirt was clean had you asked."

"I *told* you." Her daughter's voice is becoming guttural, and Dandelion thinks maybe a demon spawn is going to come out and grab her.

Silence.

"Mom, I told you."

Silence.

"Mom. Are you listening to me?"

Silence.

"You're so mean. You never do anything for me."

Silence.

Dandelion pops a pod into the coffeemaker and pushes the blinking button to brew another cup of energy. The aroma of the hot caffeinated nectar washes over her like the gentle waves of a lake lapping the shore and smooths away the hairline cracks forming in her armor. She pours in some milk and sits at the opposite end of the bar from Thistle, swipes her phone screen to begin reading the news, and ignores the dirty looks being shot at her from across the kitchen.

"Why are you ignoring me?"

"Honey, silence is an answer, and it's a powerful one."

Oh, I'm sorry, I forgot – I only exist when you need something

"Hey, Dandelion." PTA Petunia comes waltzing across the hallway as Dandelion tries to make a beeline for the toilet.

"Oh, hello, Petunia. What can I do for you?"

"Well, you know, it's almost that time of year when the PTA needs to find nominees for next year's board members."

"Uh-huh." Dandelion keeps seeing a big fat red light blinking on Petunia's face. She can also see Mags staring at her wide-eyed from across the room as if she's telepathically trying to send her a message to get the hell out of there.

"And, well," Petunia continues, "some of us were talking it over and we thought you'd be perfect to head up that process. It's not a huge commitment."

That may be true, thinks Dandelion, *but I think I'd actually rather be committed instead.* "It's so kind of you to think of me. But I'm going to have to pass," Dandelion says. To make eye contact with her friend, Dandelion cocks her head to one side of Petunia's, then winks over at Mags to let her know she received her message loud and clear.

"Really? I mean, you're usually so willing to help. You never let me down," stammers a stunned Petunia.

"Yeah. I'm not going to be able to help you with that. I'm sure you'll find another capable soul," Dandelion replies. *More like sucker.* "What about the new mom from Ghana? Wasn't she asking about getting involved?" Dandelion feels bad for throwing the other woman under the bus, but it isn't a lie. The Ghanaian woman did say she wanted to get involved. So really, she's killing two birds with one stone – dodging Petunia's request and helping the newbie become an active member of the school community.

"Well, I must admit, I'm surprised and a little disappointed, Dandelion." Petunia seems a little hurt being shot down by Dandelion. She isn't used to people saying no to her. "I assume you'll be helping with the Teacher Appreciation Pancake Breakfast next week?"

Dandelion has already started to make her way to the toilet before Petunia finishes her question, and as she opens the door, she looks back and says, "I need to check my calendar." But Dandelion already knows she's busy.

You know what that sounds like? Not my problem.

"You know Oleander, don't you, Dandelion?" says Primrose, a very timid British woman who always looks so posh. Her red hair is pulled back into a tight ponytail and her Marks & Spencer cardigan is buttoned to the top. She is standing across from Dandelion, who's having coffee with Rosey and Dahlia at a large community-style table at an outdoor café for a post-workout caffeine kick. Primrose's question isn't exactly a great conversation starter.

Dandelion hesitates then looks up from her phone with a 'why me' look on her face. "Yeah, sure. Why?"

"Well, I posted a bunch of items online for sale and Oleander said she wanted them, but I can't get in touch with her to come pick them up. She's not responding to my texts. I can see that she's read them."

"Huh. That's annoying." Dandelion isn't surprised in the very least by this tidbit of information.

"Does she pick up at school? Maybe I can catch her there."

"I think so." All these questions are making Dandelion feel squirrely; she wants absolutely nothing more to do with Oleander.

"Do you know what class her kids are in?" pecks Primrose.

Dandelion looks up at the tennis-skirt-wearing woman with a look of understanding. And then she tells a barefaced lie. "I'm sorry, but I don't."

"I just don't know what to do. I don't want to go back on my word, but I've had these items reserved for over a month. I'm trying to get ready to relocate back to London and I really need to get rid of them. It's just rude."

Dandelion stays silent and twists her lips in a 'I'm not sure what to tell you' look.

"Do you think I should repost them? Give it to the next person who raises their hand?"

Dandelion doesn't want to come off as being salty, but she really has no desire to be part of this conversation. She thinks the woman standing across from her is nice enough, but she doesn't want to be involved in her decision-making process. "Well, I mean," waffles Dandelion, "you've gotta do what's best for you." She watches Primrose's face as it struggles to cope with Dandelion's response. Primrose is clearly looking for something much less vague.

"Thanks, I think, Dandelion. Sorry, but I must run to tennis now. I'll see you around."

"I hope it works out for you," adds Dandelion as Primrose walks away. She really can't figure out why she's being thanked but feels safe knowing she's done a good job of steering clear of any Oleander-related drama – and she isn't going to feel responsible for fixing anyone else's issues.

I know, I know, I stood up for myself. I'm such a bitch.

As time passes, Dandelion begins noticing she no longer feels as if her days are spent going in circles trying to appease the masses. Yes, there are setbacks, but that's to be expected. [You're making progress, Dandie.]

Sure, she occasionally finds herself being **#*railroaded*** by Thistle and Wivi when she's not mentally prepared for whatever battle is brewing, or she catches herself rage cleaning after someone leaves a mess in the kitchen instead of telling the perpetrator to clean it up. Previously, this would've catapulted her emotional state into seek and destroy mode, taking out everything in its path, and then later, she'd sit at the mirror and be embarrassed about her childlike behavior.

PTA Petunia and her bouquet of loyal followers have noticed a difference in Dandelion's willingness to participate in their quest for school domination. Dandelion sometimes finds herself begrudgingly stuffing envelopes for an upcoming charity event after a moment of weakness, but the instances are becoming fewer and further between.

When she does commit to helping, she makes sure she puts her priorities before anyone else's.

Now and again she feels a twinge of remorse for RSVPing "no" to the women's club coffee morning again or for the way her words come over as too snappy when she speaks with someone. But hell, she's trying her best to put herself first in her world. She reminds herself to be softer and assertive, not harsh and aggressive.

Feeling like a doormat is becoming less and less of a daily reality for Dandelion. It feels like she hit the emergency stop button on a maniacal treadmill that kept increasing its speed and incline. Breaking this behavior and maintaining boundaries takes time and an enormous amount of practice. It feels good to once again be in control of how she lets herself be treated, and she isn't about to let this momentum and motivation go to waste. She's ready to keep her transition in motion but realizes she can never stop practicing what she's already learned.

#MYTHEORY

The process of creating boundaries is tough stuff. No doubt about it. Any time you try to retrain the brain or start something new — from quitting smoking to starting an exercise regime — it takes practice, determination, and discipline. Creating boundaries is no different.

I'm not a psychologist, but I do know the brain is super complex. I've read that it takes 21 days for you to make or break a habit; I've also read it takes 90 days to make a lifestyle change. I think this might be true for some people, but muscle memory works both ways. I mean, I love working out, but I also love being super lazy. Let's face it, it's pretty damn hard to be on point all the time.

I quit smoking years ago. I'll admit I didn't find it too hard to quit, but I know others who've struggled time and time again to kick the habit. I rarely have a desire to smoke. It isn't something I want to do anymore. I don't like the taste, the smell, or the way I feel the next day. But on the off chance that I do take a drag of a cigarette, I immediately remember why I quit in the first place and am instantly pissed at myself for doing it. Creating that boundary in my life was easy, but small reminders as to why I put that boundary in place help me remember why it's so important I don't get off target.

Just because you put boundaries in place doesn't mean you'll be perfect at upholding them. Even someone who's trying to quit smoking and continually caves to the cravings can keep trying to give it up. It's okay to restart things if you get off track. The important thing to remember is to not give up.

What you allow is what will continue

I had no idea I was living a life without boundaries. I thought being in constant motion was normal and that keeping the peace by making others happy at my own expense was too. Take it from me, it's no way to live. I had no idea my exhaustion was partly due to me not being in control of how I allowed others to treat me.

Once I realized how unacceptable my own behaviors were and how detrimental they were to my happiness, I was able to move forward and act swiftly to develop firm perimeters. Here are the four S's that help me keep my boundaries in focus and stop me from getting shat on.

1. **Set Expectations**
    Setting boundaries is all about creating a new precedent. For new boundaries to work, you must break the mold of the existing expectations and reinvent a new structure. This might put some people into a tailspin – you know, all those people who have been taking advantage of you for so

long – but this isn't about them or their feelings. Over time, our actions slowly turn into assumed behaviors, kind of like predictive text. I guess I can't really blame people for getting used to the way I once behaved, but it doesn't mean I can't change. Creating a boundary strives to shift those expectations. Keep in mind that when boundaries are crossed – and they will be – we need to speak up immediately. This keeps our boundaries from veering off and creating an entirely unwanted new expectation.

2. **Stop Apologizing**
   I used to find myself saying sorry or giving excuses for why I couldn't do something. It was ridiculous. The reason is no one's business but my own, and I don't need to justify my decision. I still occasionally find myself apologizing, and when I do, I stop myself mid-sentence. I also believe I should never feel guilty about my decision. If people get upset with you creating boundaries, that's just too damn bad. It's also a BIG red flag. They're upset because you are making their life harder, and they were happily taking full advantage of you being a wet noodle. Now that you've got a backbone, they can't manipulate you anymore. And it pisses them off.

3. **Start Prioritizing**
   Putting myself first is not a selfish act. It's an act of self-love and self-respect. Who says my experiences aren't just as important as everyone else's? Everyone else, that's who. I didn't do this for a long time, and I ended up being full of resentment. When I began to put myself at the top of the happiness list, it didn't mean I no longer cared about other people's level of happiness, it meant that I was now empowering myself to take care of my needs and feelings before those of others. I didn't realize my life experiences were just as important as everyone else's. I still enjoy making people feel special, but I no longer make myself

feel like shit for others to feel awesome. There's gotta be some balance.

4. **Stay Strong**
   It's so easy to get off course. We ASSes are juggling a lot of things, and it's easy to let a ball drop. It took a lot of determination to change my life. I'm still working on it every day. I can't stop working on it because it would be so easy to backslide into my old routines and habits. Muscle memory is a thing, and the body wants what the body wants — to be lazy. Don't give up on you because it's easier for everyone else. You deserve what you want just as much as anyone else. You'll thank yourself later.

Be careful how much you tolerate. You're teaching them how to treat you.

When I first began working on setting boundaries, my daughters were the first ones to feel the effects. I'm pretty sure they didn't fully grasp what was happening. I was no longer their servant and I was free of their incessant demands. I'm sure it was a shock to the system — the girls no longer had someone to place their unattainable expectations on. I mean, I'm not going to lie, I still do plenty of crap for my kids that they could do for themselves. I'm a mom; it's what I do. But I had to stop the behaviors that were making me feel terrible. I didn't want them to grow up thinking it was okay to treat people — especially their mother — in such a manner.

These changes were crafted by me and for me, but they inadvertently helped me teach a valuable life lesson to my children — those personal boundaries are essential to Mom's wellbeing, and by adhering to her boundaries, she feels respected and appreciated and is probably willing to give a little more because it isn't being demanded of her.

I must stress one point, though: sticking to these boundaries is an ongoing battle, and it's very easy to slip back into old routines. I'm human and sometimes I get tired of maintaining the boundaries with my girls. They are fierce fighters and don't give up easily, and I expect big things from them one day. Even though we have lots of mêlées – some big and some small – I can't allow myself to be a sucker. Being a sucker teaches them one of two things – either they'll assume it's okay to milk others throughout their life, or they'll think it's okay to be a pushover. And neither of those options is what I'm willing to take a chance on raising, nor am I willing to allow myself to be that person anymore. And I don't think you should either.

10

My alone time is for everyone's safety

#self-care

Don't forget to drink water and get some sun. You're basically a houseplant with complicated emotions.

"Do you ever feel like you just need a break?" Dandelion really wants to hear what her coach has to say because she always seems so together.

"Of course, we all need breaks. I take them all the time. What do you need one from?"

"*#Adulting*."

"So what's stopping you from taking one?" asks Sunny.

"Um. Well, responsibility."

"You can be responsible and still take a break."

"I don't just need a 'break' to go shopping. I need a break where I literally don't have to be responsible for anyone except myself."

"Okay."

"I need a moment in time when I don't have to make any decisions," Dandelion continues. "No figuring out what we're eating for dinner, where we're going on vacation, or who needs new school shoes. I'm peppered with random requests for utility bills from when we lived in Mexico or background checks for visa applications. I'm constantly taking mental notes to do this or pick up that, and I'm always on. My brain is so fatigued."

"Do you do a lot of *#self-care*?" asks Sunflower.

"Like manis and pedis?"

"No! Well, yes, but no. Manis and pedis can be a form of self-care, but I mean the kind where you carve out time in your life for things that matter most to you."

"I work out every day. That's important – it stops me from murdering people." Dandelion chuckles.

"Exactly. You work out to release pent-up stress and you receive energy in return from the endorphins your body creates, all the while unconsciously keeping your body fit. And it's a priority for you. It's a perfect example of self-care." Sunflower smiles as she adjusts her headset. "What else ya got?"

"I don't know… I like to read, take baths, go out with my friends." Dandelion's face is scrunched up on the side like she's thinking hard. "Does this stuff count?"

"It does, but I think you can do even better."

Dandelion feels a bit stumped and can't really go deeper.

"What about your blog? I think that's a form of self-care for you."

"Yeah. I guess it is. I do love writing it."

"Yes! Writing is an element of your self-care routine that fills your soul." Sunflower claps her hands together in excitement. "Self-care isn't just about sitting in a spa with cucumber slices over your eyes, it's about putting your wants and needs in a position of priority and making sure they're given the attention they need."

Dandelion nods. "I'm with you."

"Okay," says Sunflower. "I want you to start thinking about how you can introduce more kinds of self-care into your everyday life. It can be as little as taking ten deep breaths before going to bed or just being still for five minutes during the day to reset. Got it?"

As their session comes to an end, Dandelion signals in agreement, scribbles SELF-CARE in her notebook, and then circles it. "Yep, I've got it." Any excuse to take five minutes and do nothing sounds like something she can definitely get on board with.

Dandelion knows self-care is important but until now hasn't given it much thought. She is struggling to see past her old definition of what it is: pampering sessions full of spa treatments and cucumber water. She must retrain her brain by redefining her image of self-care. Silly as some of the things seem, she does them anyway.

Taking care of yourself doesn't mean me first, it means me too

Dandelion loves fresh flowers but sees them as an unnecessary expense, so she rarely buys them. On Monday morning while grocery shopping, she buys a big bundle of flowers for her kitchen counter. If she must spend an enormous amount of time standing there prepping and cooking, she might as well look at something that makes her *#happy*.

She's chopping vegetables at the counter when she hears her husband come through the door. "Hi, honey."

"Hey, Dand." Oak lays his laptop bag and car keys on the large granite island and makes his way around it to give his wife a kiss. He looks tired from a long day of work. "Who are the flowers from?" he asks before popping a chopped piece of carrot in his mouth.

"From me, to me," replies his wife. Her husband isn't very big on surprising Dandie with flowers; he sticks to the traditional anniversary and Valentine's Day bouquets.

"Well, that's nice of you. They're pretty." Oak walks toward the stairs untucking his plaid button-down shirt from his jeans.

"I thought so too," she says, still chopping.

"You deserve to treat yourself."

She doesn't say anything as her husband goes upstairs to change out of his work clothes. *You are so totally right, dear*, she thinks.

Just then, Thistle rounds the corner and heads to the refrigerator to grab a juice box. "Are we having people over for dinner tonight?"

The little girl's mom returns a question with another. "Why do you ask?"

"We have flowers on the counter." Thistle is the spitting image of her mother. She points at the sprigs of yellow and pink flowers.

"No. I just thought they were pretty, so I bought them for myself. They make me happy."

"I like them too. How come you never buy me flowers?" says Thistle. Her expression hardens like she might be trying to pick a fight.

"Uh, I don't know." Dandelion's a little surprised by the inquiry and isn't really sure how to respond. "How about we share them?"

"They can make us both happy," replies her mini-replica, bouncing out of sight.

The colorful arrangement not only gives Dandie a little bit of self-care, but it gives her daughter the love she needs too.

Self-care isn't selfish

When Dandelion started living in countries where domestic helpers are common, she stopped watching TV during the day. Not that she's the kind of person to sit in front of the TV for hours, but she's become very self-conscious of what the people who work in her house might assume. She assumes they think she's lazy.

Every day, Dandie eats her lunch alone in front of her laptop at the counter. There's nothing enjoyable about it, and it's become a ritual she hates. Sometimes she just wants to relax on the couch with her feet up while her family is out of the house and eat her lunch with an episode or two of whatever show needs to be binge-watched at the time. It's her only chance to control the television.

Today, though, she arrives home to a very quiet house after a morning of errands. The kids are at school, Oak's at work, the dogs are at doggie daycare, and Imbali must be in her apartment at the other end of the house eating lunch with Tamboti, the gardener who comes once a week. While running her errands, Dandelion picked up a premade butter chicken with cauliflower rice from the grocery store for her lunch. She pops it in the microwave, grabs a diet cola from the fridge, and places her laptop on the counter.

As she pulls the steamy bowl of food from the microwave, a voice in her head says, "Go sit on the couch and watch TV." Lotus knows how much her companion hates her lonely lunch routine and it's a prime opportunity to *#indulge* in some trash TV.

Dandelion doesn't dare fight with Lotus. "I guess it's now or never because I won't be able to get near that remote later," Dandelion says to herself, and she sits down in Oak's favorite spot on the sofa and turns on the television. For the next 30 minutes she treats herself to a show that makes her laugh out loud.

Just as the show's coming to an end, a voice comes from the kitchen scullery. "Hello? Girls, are you home early?" Imbali walks around the corner to find her boss sitting cross-legged on the big brown sectional looking like she's just been caught smoking in the bathroom.

"Uh. Hey, Imbali. It's just me," Dandelion says. She straightens up from her slouching comfort and starts to gather up her plate and utensils. "I just finished eating. I'll get out of your way."

"Why? This is your house." Imbali does a little circle motion with her finger. "You aren't in my way. You don't have to hide."

The woman is right. Dandelion doesn't have to hide. And so she starts eating her lunch on the sofa every day in front of the TV, just like her kids wish she'd let them do.

Going to the bathroom alone is self-care. I can't explain it, but if you know, you know.

Dandelion's lived in five rental properties during her time as an expat. She misses living in a house of her own, where she can paint walls and hang pictures without worry. As a badass who goes from rental to rental, she settles for the best available and lives with its oddities and issues.

Her current home is an uber-modern contemporary place with a blue glass front door and 15-foot ceilings. It's a lovely house for someone else.

Dandelion dislikes this house for a few reasons. First, it's impossible to heat with its high ceilings and open-plan concept, so she drags a space heater around with her all winter. Second, there's no storage space for things like Christmas decorations and suitcases, so they're stashed in closets. Lastly, none of the en suite bathrooms have doors. Yes, Dandelion is fully aware these complaints are all *#firstworldproblems*, but she feels at the age of 40 she should be able to pee in private if she chooses to. When entering any bedroom in the house, there's a chance you'll walk in on someone doing something you can't unsee. As crazy as it sounds, self-care can be as simple as peeing alone.

When Tamboti the gardener walks in on her as she's putting on a sports bra – arms up with a full frontal of the girls – Dandelion decides enough is enough. She collapses in horror and bangs her head on a cabinet door; he runs out in shame, his dark skin glowing as red as a sparkler on the Fourth of July.

One afternoon, the landlady stops over to check some issues at the house – a crack in the ceiling, a leaky pipe, birds nesting in the eaves – all things that need to be handled and paid for by the landlord. She questions everything on Dandelion's list, especially fixing the bedroom door locks.

"It never bothered me for the door not to lock," says the landlady with a heavy Eastern European accent, "and I lived here for years. Just tell your helper not to come in when the door is closed."

Don't take me for a fool, thinks Dandelion. She knows her landlady is in over her head. This is the first time she's rented out her house, and she's failed to realize that it's not for the renter to improve or tolerate issues in the house. Her tenant is a veteran badass and knows exactly how to take care of another person's home. [Look at you go, Dandelion.] *Well, you're also a divorcée with grown kids. Maybe you don't have a need to lock the door on occasion like I do.* It's kind of a snarky thought, but Dandelion really doesn't have the patience for someone questioning her desire for privacy, especially when she's paying to live in a house she doesn't own, let alone like. No expat house is perfect, but there are some things she just isn't willing to compromise on anymore.

"I'd just really appreciate it if you could send someone to check all the doors and repair the ones that aren't functioning properly. We have guests arriving in a few weeks and I bet they'd appreciate the privacy too," says Dandelion quite reasonably. Being a bitch isn't going to get her anywhere.

"Okay, but I don't think it's worth the effort."

"Thank you. I know you don't, but it's important to me. Now, why don't we go outside and look at the garden lights that aren't working? Tamboti can explain the problem." Dandelion mentally adds a tick to her win column as she shifts the conversation to the garden and heads for the patio door.

The next week a man comes to repair all the doors in the house and provides Dandelion with keys to each lock. That evening when everyone is home, she goes upstairs, locks the bedroom door, and pees in *#private* for the first time in months. She's confident no one is going to barge in to ask her where their iPad is or if they can have a snack. She considers never coming out.

You've been working on yourself and it shows

The past few months feel like a blur. Dandelion's working hard to keep up with all the lifestyle changes she's been making, and there are days when she feels like a clown on a unicycle juggling bowling pins. But it's starting to get easier.

She hears her phone make a special ding and knows exactly which group chat it's from. The text reads: "Sunday walk – clubhouse in 10." She replies with a thumbs-up emoji, and two more appear on the screen a second later.

Dandelion pops her sneakers on, grabs a baseball cap, and shouts, "I'm going for a walk." There's no response and she figures they'll call her mobile if there's an emergency. Being able to escape the house without having to answer to anyone is a rarity, so she gets the hell out of there before someone realizes Mom has an idle moment.

She jogs down the front steps and out into the warm afternoon. The sky is turning a pale pink as the sun begins to fade behind the trees, and she can hear birds chattering in the canopy of trees lining her street. As she turns the corner, Rosey approaches from her end of the neighborhood.

"What's up, chick?" Rosey's Aussie accent is thick. "I reckon these bloody mozzies are going to eat me alive." She smacks her arm. "I forgot to put repellent on."

"Oh shit. I forgot too. They're the worst." Dandelion figures she'll go home with at least one or two giant welts from the bugs that double as birds.

The two friends chat as they walk toward their meeting point to catch up with Mags and Dahlia.

Rosey volunteers to cook all the kids' dinners on Wednesdays to give her friends a break. "How's fried rice and spring rolls sound?" she asks Dandie.

"Perfect. Especially since I'm not cooking it." Dandie laughs. "Look, there's Mags."

As they approach the clubhouse, Dahlia comes through the opposite corridor and the friends head through the parking lot and onto the sidewalk.

Two by two, they walk up and down the hills for over an hour without a lull in the conversation.

"Dandie, how's your coaching thing coming along?" asks Dahlia.

"Yeah, how is it?" says Rosey, taking a sip of water from her sports bottle. "You never talk about it. Spill."

The two of them are in front of her and she is beside Mags. Dandie glances over to see if Mags is also curious, but her blue-eyed friend is looking straight ahead. Mags knows how difficult Dandie finds it to admit she's having to rely on a coach, and Dandie assumes her friend doesn't want to add any pressure to the situation.

"It's great," says Dandelion.

Mags' stoic face softens and a little smile creeps into the edges of her mouth. This friend may not be one to gush with emotions, but Dandie is totally aware of the amount of support Mags has been giving her and how she's nursed the cuts and bruises from Oleander's duping.

"I've been learning so much about myself by taking stock of how I live my life and where to focus my energy. Probably sounds hokey to you guys."

"No, it doesn't," Mags interjects. "Stop belittling your effort. Whatever you are doing is working. You've been a different person lately." Mags isn't one to mince words, so when she speaks, everybody listens. "I haven't seen you this happy in months. You've stopped taking crap from people and you're no longer doubting yourself. Now, you must accept the accolades for all your hard work. Just own it, Dandelion." [Talk about a badass.]

"She's right, Dand." Dahlia stops and turns around to face her. "I've been impressed with your determination, but you've kept this under wraps like we're going to judge you. We see the changes. You've got to feel a difference."

"I do."

Rosey smiles at Dandelion. "We're **#proud** of you. Tell us about it. I know I could use some good advice on getting my hot mess in order."

The friends continue their walk, and Dandelion tells them all about what she's been working on for the past months. Knowing they can see a difference in the way she's presenting herself makes her feel like all the hard work isn't for nothing.

She suspects Oak is also noticing differences in her. He's mentioned a couple of things in passing but said he couldn't put his finger on what exactly was different. She was less tense, more easy-going, and a bit more spontaneous – kind of like the pre-motherhood version of the woman he married. Dandelion wants to continue making significant life changes. Ones that are bold enough, so her husband won't be able to miss them.

Eventually, she'll come around and tell him what's going on inside that pretty little head of hers.

#MYTHEORY

A great example to explain self-care is charging a mobile phone. If you're like me, you charge your mobile phone every night. It's something we don't think about; we just do it. But what if we're exhausted and forget to plug it in before bed? What will happen? If it were me, I'd become a low-functioning mess of anxiety, worrying about my dwindling connection to the world. I'd switch on the low power mode function to limit my usage and reserve whatever battery is left. As stupid as it sounds, it's a terrible feeling, and I don't want it to happen – especially during a stressful situation.

The same thing happens to us when we don't recharge our batteries. We're no longer capable of firing on all cylinders because low power mode has been engaged to simply 'get by.' If we made ourselves an innate priority – which means knowing exactly where we stand on the list of attention-seeking issues: at the very top – our performance would be at a higher level because we'd be physically, mentally, and emotionally in a better place.

Girl, do it for you

Badasses, we need to stop putting ourselves last – last to sit down at the dinner table, last to pack our bag for a vacation, or last to wind down in the evening. We're consumed with making sure everyone else's batteries don't run out of juice because we don't want to deal with the disruption it causes. We think that if we keep everyone else happy, our life will be easier. And for a while it might be, but what happens when our fuel reserves turn into fumes and our world comes to a grinding halt? There won't be anything left for us or anyone else.

1. **Get over the guilt**

   There's literally nothing to feel guilty about when it comes to taking care of yourself. If we don't take care of ourselves, who the hell will? I wish there were fairy godmothers flying around waving wands and saying 'Bibbidi-bobbidi-boo!' but there aren't. The simple act of caring for ourselves allows us to nurture and grow in incredible ways. We just need to hush our inner critic and grant ourselves the freedom to take care of business. Talk about badass.

   I used to feel guilty about taking time for myself, but I got over it when I finally picked up on the fact that no one else seemed to feel guilty about doing it. I'm just as important as anyone else, and hitting a wall of depletion will put things into perspective quickly when you don't have the smallest bit of energy or desire to do just about anything. I'm sure people think my self-care routine is selfish, and if they do, well, it's none of my business what they think. I don't really share my self-care routine with others, but if you see me skiing with friends on a Thursday afternoon – you bet that's self-care. I'm worth it, and so are you.

2. **Put yourself at the top**
   When you get on an airplane and watch the video about the oxygen masks falling from the ceiling, what do they always say? "Before helping others, put your own mask on first." If you help everyone else first, you might be dead before you get a chance to put the damn thing on your face. They say it for a reason.

   When my husband traveled 85% of the time and we had a toddler and preschooler, I realized I was running on empty a lot. There just wasn't enough time in the day for me to add self-care into my routine because I was falling into bed right after the girls each night. With my husband gone so much, I didn't have someone else to step in when I needed a break, so I hired one. I found two high-school-aged sisters that loved to babysit. Twice a week, they'd take the bus to my house after school and take care of my girls for a few hours. I rarely did anything glamorous – grocery shopping, boot camp class in the park, or an occasional dinner with a friend – but those pockets of time were exactly what I needed to feel like a person again.

3. **Pencil yourself in**
   If you struggle to find time in your day to implement a little self-care, block the time in your calendar. Don't let excuses like "something came up" or "I ran out of time" be the reason you let looking after yourself slip through your fingers. You put all sorts of important reminders in your calendar, right? You don't forget to show up at the dentist

on time, do you? So don't forget your self-care either. Every Sunday evening, I take a few minutes to look at my calendar for the week. During that time, I schedule my self-care appointments — exercise, meditation breaks, meet-ups with friends, and so on — just like I would for a meeting or an appointment. Taking the extra step of adding it to my calendar makes me accountable for my wellbeing and there's less chance I'll skip or cancel it. When the reminder pops up on my screen, I don't ignore it. I get ready to tackle whatever activity I have planned for myself. When I check it off my calendar, it's proof of how much I'm showing up for myself each day.

4. **Become a creature of habit**
Creating a routine is a great way to introduce good self-care habits in your life. If you are a morning person and like to get your energy early, maybe do some stretches and breathing exercises before getting out of bed. Or, if you're a night owl, try journaling before brushing and flossing your teeth. These little self-care quickies are good add-ons to your daily routines and might eventually become second nature in your everyday life.

I love my dogs, and I walk them every day — rain, sun, or snow. I don't always look forward to it, but I'm always pleased when it's done. It gets me outside, where I breathe in the fresh air, and I fill my senses with whatever Mother Nature has up her sleeve. And I simultaneously make my dogs' day, which makes it even more worthwhile. I depend on this routine and so do my dogs. When I reach for the leashes, they know exactly what's up. It's not a chore but a happiness boost.

5. **It's a cheap high**
Self-care doesn't have to mean expensive trips to the day spa. Those are nice, but they're not always an option. There

are tons of cheap ways of adding self-care into your life. Taking 10 deep breaths to lower your heart rate before making a phone call in a foreign language to book a doctor's appointment is a form of self-care. Buying the imported yellow mustard instead of the local brand because it's familiar yet tastes the same is a form of self-care. And sitting in your car eating a donut before you pick up your kids from school is a form of self-care. Read a book, go for a walk, meditate, listen to music, take a nap... I could go on, but you get my drift. Self-care is everywhere; we just need to be more intentional with it.

I love drinking my coffee all alone before the rest of the house wakes up. It's my quiet time before my family starts their day. I wake up 30 minutes before the alarms are set to go off. Yes, I could sleep in a little bit more, but it's part of my morning routine and a priority. I get up, let the dogs out, make a cup of coffee, let the dogs in, then for 15 minutes I sit my butt on the sofa next to a happy dog and scroll through my phone catching up on social media, texts, emails, and the news. When I'm done, I'm ready and focused to tackle the day.

Self-care is how you take your power back

Isn't it funny how the idea of self-care is often confused with selfishness? Self-care is about replenishing your internal resources to be the best possible you, and selfishness is about taking from others to their detriment. To me, the difference is crystal clear. Unfortunately, the haters of the world don't comprehend the importance of putting yourself at the top of your very long list of shit that needs attention. It's probably a sign they need to mind their own damn business and work on their own self-care regimen.

Everyone needs to practice self-care because you can't pour from an empty cup, so you've got to make the choice to take the time to refill it. If we don't replenish ourselves, we'll run out of gas and everything will come crashing down. No one has the time to clean up that kind of dumpster fire. I do my best to stay focused on keeping up with my self-care and view it as random acts of kindness to myself. We do nice things for other people all the time, so why shouldn't we do it for ourselves too?

As we shift our mindset about what self-care looks like, we need to also think about what it does for us. Yes, it refuels our energy reserves and rests our weary minds. But it also strengthens us to keep forging ahead to be the best badasses we can be.

11

Being married is like having a best friend who doesn't hear anything you say

#communication

Marriage lets you annoy one special person for the rest of your life

It's 5:45 on Friday morning. Before starting the day, Dandelion already knows she isn't in the mood to cook dinner. She rolls out of bed, puts on her slippers, and goes to the kitchen for coffee. Twenty minutes later her husband comes down the stairs dressed and ready to tackle whatever is on his agenda. His blue eyes match the color of his crisp oxford shirt. He looks comfortable in his skin.

"Morning!" she says. "How does the clubhouse sound for dinner tonight? I don't feel like playing chef later, and I was going to ask Rosey and Elm if they'd be interested in joining us." She smiles, then dives into the bottom of her coffee cup.

His response is like nails on a chalkboard. "Yeah. Whatever you want."

"How's six o'clock?"

"Sure." He's packing up his laptop bag and looking for his keys. He isn't listening to her. She could've told him she was leaving him for another man and he'd have answered the same.

"Is everything okay? You're being awfully short with me," Dandelion says with a tinge of hurt and annoyance in her voice. She isn't asking for a load of attention, but she certainly doesn't deserve his gruffness. Snapdragon pops into her head checking to see if she can add any fuel to this little fire, but Dandelion shoos her away.

"I've just got a lot going on at work. I've got a big meeting today." He finds his keys under his laptop bag, grabs them, and heads for the door. "I've gotta go. I'll get to the clubhouse when I can." A minute later, the taillights of his SUV are rolling down the street.

"Okay, jackass!" she snaps. "Well, have a nice day to you too."

Dandelion picks up her phone to text Rosey about dinner. She's annoyed with her husband. How's she to know he has a big meeting at work? It's not like he ever mentions what's going on at the office. Not that she really cares, but she'd listen if he wanted to unload on her about things.

She texts her friend: "CH dinner tonight?"

There's an immediate response: "Yes, I can't be bothered to cook."

Dandie pecks at her phone: "Reservation's at 6."

"Rosé at 4:30. See you then."

Dandelion and her friend are completely in sync. One needn't say much to the other to know exactly what they're thinking. It's like they're speaking *#shorthand*, but it isn't short in a negative way. It is precisely the opposite of what she feels with Oak lately.

The sun is setting pink and orange over the trees and the lawn in front of the clubhouse is full of kids playing when Oak finally arrives. He finds his wife and friends already indulging in the weekend fun at an outdoor dining table.

"Hey, mate. Glad you could join us," says Elm, handing his friend a beer from the ice bucket on the table. "The cricket's on tomorrow. Keen for an afternoon in front of the patio telly? I'm going to let Spruce and Chestnut know too."

The men begin planning their Saturday afternoon cricket-watching, and the evening continues without a hitch. Dandelion sweeps this morning's feelings of annoyance under the rug and lets them sit there waiting to be revisited.

Marriage tip: your wife won't start an argument if you're cleaning

Dandelion realizes she's almost two-thirds through her coaching process and is feeling so much more confident than when it started. She hasn't showered, her hair looks a mess, and she has no makeup on. But she doesn't care. Not having herself together would have previously made her feel incredibly self-conscious in front of Sunny, but now she owns it. *Who's the badass now?*

The computer begins to ring, and she clicks the green icon to accept the call. She sees herself side by side with her coach. One of them has a head full of waves and lipstick; the other is sporting a messy bun and gym clothes. Neither of them cares what the other one looks like.

There's a plaintive "Hey, Dandie, how are you?" from the computer speaker.

"Good, and you?"

"You know, I'm feeling kind of under the weather today. But I'm trying to power through." Sunflower picks up her glass of water and takes a giant gulp. "I've got ginger and lemon in here." She points to the pitcher of water on her desk.

"Maybe you need to make a little time for a self-care break today. How about a nap?" Dandelion's in a good mood and can't resist schooling the teacher. Lotus is feeling all the feels.

"I know, right? A nap sounds amazing. Maybe I can squeeze one in after we're done today." She takes another sip of water. "Enough about me; this is your time. Tell me, what's going on with you?"

Dandelion sits quietly for a few seconds, deliberating about how she wants to structure her thoughts. She's been thinking a lot about her recent interactions with Oak. They seem strained, yet she doesn't feel like her marriage is in trouble in the least. He seems distant. Not in a 'I don't love you' kind of way, more a 'something's taking up a lot of headspace' kind of way – like there isn't any room left for her in his head. She doesn't think he's quite recognizing all of the hard work she's doing for their life, and she's becoming a little ***#resentful***. She doesn't want to be bitter but can't help it.

"Something's up with my husband and me." She says it so matter-of-factly that it's like she's already accepted the problem and is ready to just dive in and fix it.

"Okay. So, you're going to have to give me more than that short statement because my thoughts are going in a million directions right now." Sunflower has a real look of concern on her face.

"We're not on the brink of divorce, no one is cheating, and we're still having sex." Dandelion smiles and needs to make Sunflower know her marriage isn't on the verge of collapse. "I feel like I don't know what's going on with him. He seems closed off and a bit emotionally shut down lately. It's frustrating me and making me resent him. I've made many sacrifices over the years, and I just want to feel like he acknowledges and appreciates it. It's not like *I'm* the reason we moved 10,000 miles from home."

"I have to stop you for a second. Do you hear yourself? You are a different person today. Your confidence is on fire. You have come such a long way from all those months ago. You know exactly what your problem is and are locked in on fixing it. I love this." Sunflower is dancing in her seat. "Okay, sorry. I just had to point that out and celebrate you for a second. Have you tried talking to him about it?"

"Well, sort of. But it ends in a passive-aggressive argument. We're not the kind of people who have knockdown drag-out fights. We just get pissy with each other and walk away without any resolution. Then we act like it never happened." She stares at the screen. "I know, it's really adult of us." Dandelion rolls her eyes.

Sunflower is typing notes into a shared document. She stops and looks straight into the computer camera. "Communicating with your partner can be scary because we don't know how they are going to respond." This statement is so real and raw. "There are lots of ways to do it delicately without being condescending. You just have to be brave enough to hear what the other person is going to say."

Is Dandelion **#brave** enough to hear the other side of the argument without being defensive? Frankly, she has no choice because she can't continue to allow her feelings to be pushed aside for the benefit of his. They're married, for fuck's sake. Marriage isn't easy, but it's worth it. She loves her husband and herself enough to know she must be bold as brass.

For the rest of the session, Sunflower helps guide Dandie to better understand how open **#communication** can be conversational and not confrontational. Dandelion sees that her previous tactics may have unintentionally provoked a negative response from her husband. Her head and her heart are in the right place, but her delivery is way off.

"Remember," Sunny cautions Dandelion, "don't shoot from the hip. Take time to think about what you want to say, and find the right time to say it. I know you can do this, Dandelion. Be brave."

I am yours. No refunds.

Dandelion mulls over the discussion she had with her coach. She wants to make sure she has a firm grasp of what to say and how to say it. Knowing the outcome she desires won't be achieved by coming at her husband with guns blazing, she makes notes, wracks her memory for examples, and steadies herself for his response.

One night after the girls have gone to sleep, she finds her husband reading the news on his tablet. No distractions, no time limit, and no current stress. "Hey," she says. "You got a minute?"

"Yeah. What's up?" Oak puts his tablet on the sofa cushion next to him. "Or should I say, what's wrong?" He's smiling but looks a little worried.

Don't be an idiot, Oak. "I don't know," she says. "You tell me." Dandie takes a seat opposite him on their sectional sofa. Enough distance between them, but close enough to be across from each other and talk without raising their voice. She's wringing a piece of paper in her hand – her notes.

"Huh?" Her husband looks confused.

"You seem distant lately. I need to know if everything's alright between us." She's trying to keep her emotions from escaping her eyes. "We barely talk."

"Everything is *fine*."

Eww, he used the word 'fine.'

Oak reaches for his tablet. "We're good, nothing to worry about."

His wife knows if she lets him swipe the screen to open the tablet, the conversation will be over. "Oak, I'm not *fine* with the way things are right now." She isn't sure where the strength is coming from, but her words are bold enough to get his attention.

"What do you mean?" He puts the tablet in his lap.

"It bothers me that you and I don't talk anymore. Or that you're short with me, like last Friday when I tried discussing dinner plans with you. You just blew me off. It made me feel like I'd done something to trigger you. But I don't know how because you never say anything to me." Her voice is quivering, but she's doing an excellent job at not sounding overly emotional. "When you don't engage with the kids or me, I begin to resent you." She's said it.

His eyebrows shoot up. "You resent me?"

"Sometimes." She isn't proud of it, but she's proud of herself for admitting it.

"Why?"

"Well, I feel like you're shutting me out. You talk to everyone else with ease, but with me, you just stay quiet. There's nothing like hearing secondhand information from your friends about something your husband said." She can feel her heart rate getting faster. [Calm the fuck down, Dandelion.] "At the very least, I want to know how your day was."

"Dand, I appreciate your effort. I really do. But when I get home from work, the last thing I want to do is talk about work."

"But…" She stops herself. She needs to let him speak.

Oak rubs his forehead and then continues. "I talk to people all damn day – in meetings, on the phone, at lunch. Hell, I can't even walk to the bathroom without someone stopping me to talk about some urgent issue."

"I never thought about it that way." Her strength is wavering. [Do not quit now.]

"I'm sorry that I'm not super talkative when I get home, but I just want to decompress and relax." His tone has turned a bit sour. "I want to leave work at work."

"Okay. So, you need to decompress in the evenings and not talk about work. That's fair enough. I just assumed you were mad at me for some reason and that work was more important."

He nods. "I get that. Do you know my favorite time of the day?"

Dandelion shakes her head.

"My drive home from work. You want to know why?"

She shrugs her shoulders.

"Because I don't have to talk to anyone. I don't have to think about solving problems, and I can't respond to anyone's requests. I sit in traffic feeling carefree. There's nothing to do but sit and wait for the car in front of me to move forward." [Who'd have guessed? Oak has his own self-care routine too.]

"I hear you. But unlike you, I don't talk to people all day, and I spend a lot of time alone." Dandelion knows she has to clearly state her needs. "I need to interact with an adult at the end of the day. Talking with people feeds my energy." She pauses. "So, how do we both get what we want?"

For the next hour, the couple sit together discussing their current state of the union. They listen to each other's concerns, ask plenty of questions, and come to mutual understandings that wouldn't have been reached if she hadn't had the guts to speak up. Dandelion shouldn't be scared to talk to her husband. He's her partner, the guy she loves.

She makes a promise not to bombard him with questions when he walks in the door. Instead, she'll give him time to unwind and settle into the evening. He'll be sure to ask her how her day has been and see if she needs his input on anything. She'll ask for help – because he isn't a mind reader. He'll be better at recognizing her signals so he can jump in and take over. There are lots of these types of little things that will make their relationship stronger. From now on, they can be open and honest with each other when it comes to how they feel.

"So, um, Dand…." Oak has a look of guilt on his fair-skinned face. "Since we're talking about how things will look in the future… what do you think about the idea of living in Switzerland again?"

"I'm sorry – what?"

Oh boy, #herewegoagain.

#MYTHEORY

Wouldn't it be great if we lived in a world where our partner or spouse knew precisely what we were thinking? Well, maybe not all the time. I don't really want mine to know how frequently I contemplate smothering him with a pillow in his sleep because of his snoring. But how cool would it be if he just knew I wanted him to walk the dogs or pick up milk from the store on his way home from work? As much as I wish he was a mind reader, he's not. So I've got to make it evident to him by "using my words," as I used to tell my daughters when they were little.

In the early years of parenting, I can recall countless times when my daughters were super frustrated while trying to express themselves. They'd be wailing with snot dripping down their faces, and I would kneel in front of them in my own frustrated state because I couldn't understand what the hell they wanted. I used to say repeatedly, "Use your words." If they could say one or two words to give me a hint, like "more milk," I could probably fix the situation. The same holds true for adults. If we explain what we need, we just might get it.

Sometimes I wonder how you put up with me. Then I remember — I put up with you too. So we're even.

Being able to correctly articulate what we want to say takes practice. I personally struggle a lot with this. Sometimes I get it right but sometimes I don't — and those are the situations I can learn from the most. How could I have dealt with that differently? Maybe it was terrible timing, I misread his mood, or I was a little too assertive. I am never going to be perfect, but I can try to be better than terrible.

1. **Don't shoot from the hip**
   Before broaching a difficult topic with my husband, I do myself a favor and have a good think. Taking time to think through the issue helps clarify what I hope to accomplish with the discussion. I prepare myself for the conversation by naming my feelings and identifying examples of what upsets me instead of just blaming him without evidence. Having a little prep session to practice the conversation in my head and work through possible scenarios helps keep me focused and unflustered when it's really happening.

2. **Timing is everything**
   If I engage in a tough talk with my spouse while I'm hot under the collar, it'll most likely lead to a shouting match — at least that's my experience. So I allow myself to cool down and compose myself before engaging with him. But I don't let the problem irritate me for too long; I don't want it to get worse. I also find a moment that's calm and unhurried. Before waking the kids up for school or right before meeting friends isn't ideal. It creates a hard break and I'll never get the original momentum back when we try to revisit the conversation later.

3. **Shut your trap**
   Yes, I might've been the brave one to start the conversation, but sadly — I say that jokingly — my husband deserves to be heard too. So I do my best to be an active listener and try not to interrupt him when it's his turn to cross-examine me. When he's finished, I repeat in my own words what I heard him say to make sure I've understood properly. Being a good listener also lets your spouse know you respect their thoughts too. So zip it!

I believe taking time to prepare for hard conversations can be beneficial, and I don't just apply these tools when communicating with my husband. They are universally useful.

You'll be more comfortable and confident with your delivery. It may not be easy, but having your thoughts, emotions, and timing aligned means you're less likely to veer off the course you intend to go down. With a little practice you'll organize yourself more quickly and execute things with more poise because you'll have already worked out what you want to accomplish.

Never laugh at your wife's choices. You're one of them.

Communication is a delicate little trickster. Suppose I'm not careful with my words or the way I approach a situation. I may really bungle things up. One little misstep can create significant communication barriers or shut the conversation down completely. I didn't think having a challenging conversation with my husband, the man I love and trust, would be such a big hurdle to clear. Except it was because I was avoiding it at all costs – and my happiness with it.

For far too long, I let little issues that were bothering me fester. They began to gnaw away at my core and caused resentment to develop like a slow-growing tumor. When it was time for me to say something, I was too afraid to discuss it with my husband; I was petrified of facing his truth. Did he think I was being a bitch? Most likely at one point or another. Was he frustrated with the way I dealt with things? Maybe. Sometimes. Was I doing a good job at expressing my needs? Clearly not.

I'm amazed I was ever afraid of what my husband might say to me, especially when I didn't feel overly vulnerable about our marriage. Relationships are funny things, and even though we might be linked to our partners for decades, we still want them to like us and think we're amazing all those years later. It's hard to hear the not so wonderful things, but marriage is a long journey with bumps, twists, and the occasional U-turn. Being a badass isn't just about holding on tight and enjoying the ride. It's also grabbing the toolbox when you get a flat tire and working together with your spouse on the side of the road to fix it.

12

True friends say good things behind your back and bad things to your face

#friends

Just remember: if we get caught, I'm deaf and you don't speak English

Not Switzerland again. Dandelion can't sleep. It's like there's a boom box in her head that's stuck on repeat. Snapdragon and Lotus are fighting for control of Dandelion's state of mind. In her core, Dandelion knows this is the right move for her husband's career and a great opportunity for her family. Lotus is happy knowing Dandie isn't blinded by Snapdragon's powerful persuasion. Does Dandelion know it's the right next step? Yes. Is she excited about it? No. It's a draw of wills.

The idea of moving back to where her expat life began isn't giving her the warm and fuzzies. It'll be different this time: her kids are much older, she'll be moving to the German-speaking area, and she'll know how to handle the ups and downs of expat life much better than she did the first time. But is she ready to move on and start over again? Dandie loves her life in South Africa. Her entire family loves their life in South Africa – right down to the dogs. This move isn't going to be easy.

Dandelion's supposed to keep this giant elephant of information a secret, but she must tell someone. She picks up her phone, opens the messaging app, and selects Mags' name. Her thumb darts around the screen and types, "I'm moving to Switzerland."

Mags is the perfect person to tell. Between the two of them, she and Dandie have shared more confidential info than the CIA and Interpol combined. When Dandelion found out she was moving from Mexico City to Johannesburg, she leaned on Magnolia for support. Magnolia, in turn, told Dandelion her biggest secret: that she wouldn't be alone in South Africa because she was coming with her. Talk about a shit ton of serendipity.

Three little dots. Mags is typing. "OMG. You can't leave me yet. Where? When?"

"Zug. No clue. No details." She has no more intelligence to offer up.

"Where the hell is Zug?"

"30 mins outside Zurich. Had to look it up on map. FML." Dandelion has never heard of Zug either. "Not official or announced. Put in your vault."

"Under lock and key. Promise."

Trusting she needn't worry about her news being leaked, Dandelion feels temporarily freed from the burden of her secret. Dandie knows Mags will tell her husband, Chestnut, but it'll go no further than that. *#expatfriends* are good at keeping *#expatsecrets*.

"Told the others yet?" Mags messages.

"Nope." Dandelion isn't looking forward to having that conversation with her friends. She knows they'll ultimately be supportive because moving and leaving people is part of expat life, but that doesn't make it any easier. She types, "Will drop hints at book club," and presses the send button.

Months ago, Mags announced that her family would be moving to Buenos Aires at the end of the school year, so the group of friends has had time to accept their buddy's leaving them. It's weird that she knows where and when she's moving so far in advance. As experienced expats, the friends are used to saying hello and goodbye to fellow nomads. It's the shitty reality of expat friendships.

There's a final message from Mags. "At least Dahlia and Rosey will have each other."

Dandelion takes solace in this and types her reply. "Exactly."

I did not see that coming

"Did anyone actually read the book I picked this month?" Dahlia's looking around the table for some semblance of a yes, but every one of them is obviously a no. "Begonia? Daisy? Poppy? I give up. You guys pick one next time." She flips her besties off and throws her hands up in defeat at the rest of the group.

Not even Poppy, who is a voracious reader, finished this month's selection. "It was a little deep for me," she admits. "I couldn't get past chapter four. It was a bit depressing."

"Sorry," says Dandelion, "but I have a hard time with historical dramas when I have zero knowledge of the events they chronicle." She hates telling her friend she doesn't like her selection, but hey, at least she's being honest. If you can't be honest with your friends, then they aren't really your friends.

The book discussion comes to a quick close and the group of women disband to grab food and drink refills. Dahlia, Rosey, Mags, and Dandie are left sitting in their seats.

"Since no one read the book," says Rosey glancing at Dahlia, "I'll let you in on some news." She pauses for effect. "I'm moving home!" Her face lights up with excitement that hasn't been there in a while.

"I'm sorry... what?" Dahlia is fumbling to find words. "Did you just say you're moving back to Oz?"

"Shut. Up!" Mags' jaw looks like it's come unhinged. "Seriously?"

"Yeah. Elm got a great offer in Sydney. We're leaving next month." Rosey is beaming like a neon sign. She's wanted to go back to Australia for a while and couldn't look happier.

Magnolia shoots Dandelion a knowing look and Dandelion mouths "FUCK" back at her. If Rosey is leaving too, that means Dahlia's going to be a lone wolf. The last woman standing. The sole member of their little gang to be left behind.

"Sydney is going to be amazing," exclaims Magnolia. "But it's so fast. Why are you leaving so quickly?"

"Well, we thought about it," says Rosey, "and with returning to the Southern Hemisphere school schedule versus the international school schedule, we need to get the kids back as soon as possible since the new school year has already started. It's only fair to them." Between the smiles and chatter, Rosey's taking mouthfuls of risotto. "Plus, we don't have to deal with any immigration stuff, so there's no extra delays."

"Wow, Rosey. That's incredible news," says Dahlia. She looks over at Dandelion. "I guess it's just you and me now, kid." She puts her arm around Dandie and squeezes her in a one-armed hug full of gladness and comfort, knowing she still has a sidekick to pal around with.

Not fully sure how to respond to her friend, Dandelion manages to squeak out a "Yep, just you and me." There's no way she can drop any hints about a possible move to Switzerland now. Time to **#keepyourmouthshut**. Not wanting to dwell on the subject for too long, Dandelion shifts the conversation back to Rosey. "Well, I guess we're just going to have to make the next month one to remember. Eh, Rosey?"

Rosey lifts her glass and motions to Dandie. "Chin-chin, friend. I'll drink to that."

Sometimes I wonder if this is all happening because I didn't forward that email to 10 people

"Oh, no. What's wrong?" Sunflower can tell her client isn't at the top of her game today.

"Two things. I just found out one of my closest friends is moving next month, and Oak told me we're moving back to Switzerland." Dandelion shows her resting bitch face.

"Ugh. Yeah, it's so hard when friends leave. But I think I'm more alarmed about your reaction to moving to Switzerland." Sunflower's head is tilted and her lips are pursed.

"I have zero desire to move right now." Flashbacks of her time in Geneva zoom into her mind. "Maybe it's because I know what I'm getting into."

"It won't be as bad as you think, but I understand how you feel."

"It's cold. It's cloudy. It's rigid. It's—"

"Beautiful," says Sunflower cutting her off. "And clean and safe and located in the heart of Europe."

"And expensive, and I'm required to learn German, and hiking clothes are considered high fashion. It'll never feel like home."

"Well, you've got a very glass-half-empty attitude today."

"I know. I'm sorry. I'm a total downer right now, but I can't help it." Dandelion looks away from the screen and out her office window. The tall palm trees are swaying and the sun is shining brightly. *Take a mental picture of that view because it won't look like that in Switzerland.* She's having a *#pityparty* for herself.

"You know this is a chance for growth, right?" Sunflower has her coach hat on tight this morning.

"I'm listening." Dandelion's waiting for her to say something like "turn that frown upside down" so she can hang up.

"Well, coincidentally, you've moved into the next phase of your coaching process. Ready or not, it's time for Busting ASS." She shakes her head like she's headbanging at a 90s grunge gig. "This is the fun part."

The trainee isn't sure she's ready for a next phase. There's a lot of new information already floating around her pretty little head. "So, what now?"

"Now we focus on what you want your life to look like – setting new goals, dreaming about what you want to do next. You're literally starting with a clean slate. Anything is possible. Think about what your ideal life would look like."

Dandelion shoots to images of herself on a beach with an umbrella drink and a stack of books and then shoots back to reality. "Honestly? I just want to be happy." It's the truth, and as she explains to Sunflower, she now knows she doesn't long to have a J-O-B tying her to commitment after commitment, and she sure as hell doesn't want to feel obligated to prove her worth.

"Dandelion, you're an interesting client." Sunflower is smiling at her. "I love that you're so comfortable with being honest." Dandelion's made Sunflower fully aware of what she doesn't want, but it doesn't stop her coach from digging further. "Obviously, I want you to be happy. But what else?"

"I want to be fulfilled and live with intention alongside people who make me feel good about being me. And I want to write. I want rich experiences—"

"Where's all this come from?" says Snapdragon suddenly, but Dandelion dismisses her with the look she gives her girls when she can't yell at them in public.

"Alright. Now we're getting somewhere." Sunflower looks very proud of her student. She's told Dandelion several times that she has the power to figure out exactly what she wants out of life, and Dandelion's last statement proves she was right.

"We don't have to dive deep into all of this dreaming stuff right now," Sunny continues, "so let's put a pin in that for the moment." She shifts in her seat to get comfortable. "It sounds like you've been blindsided by this move to Switzerland, and I know you have a very tight bond with your close friends. What will help you get through the not so fun process of having to say goodbye?"

"I don't know." Dandie really doesn't know. She's just tired of making new friends, and she's really hit the jackpot with the ones she's got. "The idea of starting all over again is getting to me. I hate the loneliness bit at the start of a new move."

"Saying goodbye is hard. You realize it's a grieving process, right? You're allowed to be sad."

"Yes. It just sucks. I know I'll eventually make new friends and create a good life in Switzerland." It's not as if her life in Joburg would be the same with Mags and Rosey both leaving. "We'll all be starting over in our own way."

"Very true. So, what can you do to help yourself and your friends over the coming months?" Sunflower is making Dandelion dig for the answers.

"Be there for one another like always?"

"Yep. Tell them how much you love them, and be the best friend you can be. Even though you won't see them all the time anymore, they'll know you've got their back wherever in the world they land."

Dandelion figures this is advice Sunflower may have given herself a time or two.

"It's not goodbye," says Sunflower, "it's see you later."

All you need is love and understanding

"Babe, I need to tell my friends we're moving." Dandelion's lying in bed while Oak brushes his teeth. She's picking at her cuticles, a nervous habit she's had since childhood.

"Dand, you know my new job hasn't been announced yet. You can't go around telling the world." Her husband sounds exasperated. "What's the big deal waiting a few more weeks?" He just doesn't understand.

"I need to tell Dahlia. I'm not worried about the others; they've all got one foot out the door already." [Um, hate to remind you, but one of them already knows anyway.] She's on the verge of peeling a big piece of skin off her thumb, and it's going to hurt like hell if she doesn't stop. "You don't know what it's like to lose all of your friends and be left behind."

Dandelion thinks she's right. She can't be certain, but she's pretty sure her husband doesn't feel the serious pangs of despair when saying goodbye to friends. Oak's the kind of guy who doesn't need a lot of friends. He's social and outgoing but is happy with just a few buddies who he can call if he wants to go to a rugby match or for a bike ride. And he's quite content with not being around anyone at all too. Most of the time, Dandie's the one who manages his social network – the husbands of her friends become his friends. Obviously, it doesn't always work to his advantage, but he's never the one making social connections for both of them. It's been this way since they got married.

"Keeping this secret is obviously bothering you," acknowledges Oak. "Our friends won't be broadcasting it to the masses, so you can tell them. Just remember to ask them not to tell anyone else." He bends over and kisses his wife on the forehead. "And stop picking your cuticles."

Dandelion gets out of bed and walks to the bathroom sink, where she keeps her nail clippers. "Thanks, Oak. I just need to talk about this with them. It's big for both of us, but it's different for me. I'm not taking a job at a place where everyone already knows who I am. I'm starting from the beginning again." She clips the piece of hanging skin, then rubs her thumb over it to make sure she's taken care of the problem completely. "I'm just anxious."

"I know you are. Believe it or not, I am too."

Later that afternoon, during a Sunday walk, Dandelion musters up the confidence to tell her friends she's leaving. The four friends converge at their usual meeting place like a Swiss train that pulls into the station on time.

Much of the conversation is focused on Rosey's impending departure; it's a mere three weeks away. She tells them that the movers are due to arrive the week after next and that they plan to stay in a hotel until they head off. Dandelion doesn't want to steal the attention, but she needs to share her news.

"So, ugh," she says, interrupting the conversation, "I've got a little announcement."

Dahlia, who is walking in front of Dandelion, looks over her shoulder and says, "Well, we know you're not pregnant. So what? Are you moving too?"

"Actually, yeah." Her jaw is set like she's bracing for a punch to the mouth. "To Switzerland."

"You're fucking kidding me, right?" All of a sudden, Dahlia's no longer her chipper-sounding self. "Fuck me."

Mags' eyes dart between Dahlia and Dandelion. "Hey, we're across the way from the clubhouse. Why don't we all go grab a cold drink."

Rosey and Mags lead the way while the other two trail behind.

"This sucks," Dahlia says. "I mean, I'm happy for you guys, but it sucks." She forces a smile, but her eyes are welling up with tears.

"I don't really have too much of a choice," says Dandie. She looks deeply into Dahlia's puddled eyes. "It's just part of expat life. And you're right. It does suck." Dandelion grabs Dahlia's hand and pulls her toward the clubhouse doors. "Let's go drown our sorrows. And by the way, I know I just dropped a major bomb on you, but we've still got to get Rosey's send-off planned."

"Oh, don't you worry," says Dahlia. "I've got it all figured out." Dahlia always has a grand idea up her sleeve.

Cultivating friendships is like tending a garden – sometimes you gotta get rid of the weeds

The ladies decide the best way to bid their friend farewell is a final trip to the karaoke bar for an evening of shenanigans. They rent the back room of the bar and invite all Rosey and Elm's friends and acquaintances. There are loads of people there – some who Dandelion only knows in passing and a few she's never seen before. The room's filled with the sound of laughter and terrible singing.

From the corner of her eye, Dandelion sees Oleander saunter past the bar in a coral frock that billows as she moves. Oleander walks straight up to Rosey and interrupts her conversation, creating an awkward situation. *Isn't that **#typical**.* Dandelion holds her giant gin goblet up to her face and watches Oleander work the room. One by one Oleander ticks off her hellos and makes her presence known. *Thank God I don't have to deal with her anymore*, thinks Dandelion, but as soon as she turns to head for the bathroom, she's waylaid by Oleander.

"Hey, Dandie." Oleander's tone is cordial but sounds forced. "Haven't seen much of you lately."

That's the point of avoiding you, and don't call me Dandie. "Oh, hello, Oleander. Yeah, it's been a while." She isn't in the mood to engage with this crackpot but figures she'll get it over with now. "That color looks nice on you." At least she remembers her manners to **#killherwithkindness**.

"Oh, thanks. I bought it at a boutique on Bond Street. Have you ever heard of Bond Street? It's a high-end shopping district in London." Oleander can be so condescending, and she doesn't wait for a response. "And I'm doing great. I've been so busy. I'm starting a new project, but I can't talk about it just yet. I'm still working out the kinks."

Dandelion can tell she's skimming the crowd behind her.

Oleander leaves enough low-hanging fruit in front of Dandelion to feed an entire troop of spider monkeys, but Dandelion doesn't take the bait. "Wow. Good luck with that."

An uncomfortable pause floats between them, but Dandelion holds her eye contact. There's literally nothing else she can think of saying to this woman. *Why is she even here? She doesn't even like Rosey.* "You'll need to excuse me, you caught me on my way to the ladies' room." And without hesitation, Dandelion leaves her ex-pal standing at the bar alone and heads into the haven of the toilet. Oleander looks stunned, or maybe she's just gotten her Botox topped up.

Dandelion uses the sanctuary of the ladies' room to fix her face and compose herself. With that little meeting behind her, she figures she doesn't have to worry about dealing with Oleander again for the rest of the night. The universe isn't that cruel. She sweeps her lips with pink shimmer. She can hear the faint sound of Neil Diamond playing in the distance and knows that Rosey's husband, Elm, is the soloist belting out the lyrics. She exits the toilet and finds her friends gathering around the stage and singing along in unison. "Sweet Caroline… ba, ba, ba…."

This makes her smile. The comradery this group shares fills her soul to the brim. At that moment, she knows that even though their bond of sisterhood is to be burdened by distance, they'll remain the confidants she can lean on in times of despair and celebrate with in times of joy. She might be alone in Switzerland, but she'll never be alone in friendship.

As the evening is winding down and the guests are getting into their taxis, Dandelion is approached again by Oleander. This time her demeanor is different: it's relaxed due to the gin flowing through her veins, but it's spiteful too. "Did you ever get my text? My cell phone broke, and I lost all my texts. So I never knew if you responded."

Your cell phone broke, and you lost your texts. Right.

Immediately, Dandelion knows the text in question – a nasty little message sent months ago, meant to fuck with Dandelion's mind.

It had been the last exchange between the two of them. *She knows I read the dumb message,* thinks Dandelion. *Can't the woman just #letitgo? What's the point of rehashing the same conversation over and over?*

"Do you mean the one where you told me again that people think I'm cold and unfriendly? The one that was meant to intimidate me? The one that was meant to make me feel bad about myself? Yes. I read it. I didn't think it deserved a response." Dandelion seems to have grown a couple of inches by the end of her short speech. "I'm done talking about this shit. You need to get over yourself and move on without me in your life." She turns on her heel.

"Don't you walk away from me," Oleander demands.

"Why not? I'm giving you another chance to put a knife in my back." Dandelion has no more fucks to give when it comes to Oleander. "We are done."

A few feet away, Rosey and Elm are watching this live interpretation of *Masterpiece Theatre* unfold. Rosey's close enough to step in if the claws come out. But she's glad to see Dandelion keeping a cool head as she puts Oleander back in her place. When Dandelion brushes past her, Rosey quietly cheers her friend with a "Bravo! Bravo!" and then quickly moves past her husband in Oleander's direction. "Hey, Oleander. I think it's time for you to be on your way now."

Oleander looks over at Rosey with venom in her eyes. "You're all just a bunch of bitchy trailing spouses with nothing better to do than go to the gym and drink mimosas." She points in the direction Dandelion walked away. "And that one, she's the ringleader. You're always trying to protect your private little gang of cool girls. You wouldn't know how to be inclusive if you tried."

"We let you in the door tonight, didn't we? And look where that got us." Rosey is enjoying this little scene. "Dandelion tried to be your friend, but you managed to fuck that one up all on your own. Don't blame us for your bad judgment."

Elm brings his wife a fresh G&T and she kisses him instead of saying thank you.

Oleander tries a rebuttal, but out of nowhere, Dahlia chimes in. "Why'd you show up here tonight anyway? To make this little scene? Dandelion's smarter than you give her credit. That's why she doesn't engage with your lame attempts. She knows exactly what fuels you. There's no need to protect her from you. She's too classy to stoop to your level of bullshit and schoolyard games." She stops to take a sip of her drink before delivering the final blow. "The door" – she points to the exit – "is over there."

Dandelion has no idea her friends have been defending her honor. Instead, she's on stage singing terribly out of tune alongside Mags and wondering where the other two pieces of her posse are hiding. She thinks they're missing out on the fun, but they are exactly where they're supposed to be. Her friends always have her back and she has theirs in return. That's the point of friendship. The song ends and the singers exit the stage to find the other half of their small gang sitting at a table waving them to come over and join them. All together in the corner booth, the friends laugh and cry their way through the next couple of hours before the bartender announces last call.

"I'm so lucky to have found all of you," says Dandelion. "I don't know what I'll do without you."

"What do you mean without us?" says Dahlia. "You can't get rid of us. I need places to escape to without my family, and you guys are my destinations – this ride ain't over yet."

Six months from now, they'll be thousands of miles apart. No longer close to each other. They have been there for each other in the darkest of times and in the most exciting of moments. Holidays, birthdays, and random Tuesday afternoons. They've shared laughs, tears of loss, and their biggest worries. Long, lazy afternoon lunches by the pool with their husbands and kids flood their memories, and cozy winter talks by the fire fill their souls.

Their connection is unbreakable, and no distance can take that away from them. Dandelion will be left with no regrets when it comes to her anchors. She's given them nothing but her true self and they've taught her what real friendship is in return.

#MYTHEORY

I'm a person who thrives on human connection – but on my own terms. Sometimes I crave being around people, and other times, I can't be bothered because I just need to be alone. I'm a self-proclaimed ambivert, so I need both kinds of stimulation. One point to keep in mind when I'm surrounded by others is this – it's not just *any* people, it's *my* people. The ones who get me. The ones who don't walk away when things get hard. The ones who know whether I need vodka or wine. In other words, the best kind of friends a girl can ask for.

We'll be best friends forever because you already know too much

I give myself kudos for finding my people. In fact, I'm still finding them, and I'll continue finding them until I'm old and gray. But damn did it take a lot of time, patience, and grit to get to this point. I've had to kiss a lot of frogs in a lot of places to find a clutch of fab friends. You must put in the hard work sorting through individuals that come into your life and have an impact on you.

Obviously, not every friendship will have the same level of closeness, and it doesn't mean you won't be friends with lots of people. But when you've found someone who's worthy of joining your small girl gang, you're opening yourself up to being vulnerable. This is something I don't take lightly. It's not that you aren't authentic with others, but I know I'm a hell of a lot more exposed emotionally with my people than I am with those who haven't scratched the surface of my crazy.

Here are a few key things I try to remember when cultivating friendships.

1. **Don't force it**
   I know you'll have seen this quote: "Friendship is like a fart. If you have to force it, it's probably shit." It couldn't be truer. It's like dating — if there isn't a connection, there isn't a connection. You wouldn't date someone who didn't spark excitement or desire, right? So why would you keep trying to be friends with someone who doesn't do it for you?

   Also, sometimes your people are not the people you think you're supposed to be friends with, and that's okay. On the surface, the pretty brunette you met at the gym who has kids the same age as you might seem like a good fit. But after you try to connect over vegan poke bowls, you find her to be self-absorbed, boring, and hungry. It's okay to just be friendly and not besties. It doesn't mean you'll write them off from your life, but they probably won't be your plus one.

2. **Be choosy**
   Being selective when deciding who you're going to spend your valuable time with and who you let into your inner circle is in my opinion completely acceptable and smart. For me personally, I tend to take a little time to truly open up to people. I mean, I'm an open book — a total stranger can ask me about my child birthing experiences and I'll give them all the gory details — but to get to my innermost thoughts... that takes time. If people think that's bitchy, then so be it — they clearly aren't my kind of people. It's your right to choose who to let into your personal space. As far as I'm concerned, they've gotta earn it.

3. **Some people are meant to teach you a lesson**
   As I mentioned in *Chapter 3*, sometimes our judgment gets clouded when we're choosing who we let into our lives. It's happened to me a few times, and well, it's a real bitch to deal with in the moment, but I've come to grips with the fact

that sometimes the universe needs to teach (or reteach) me a lesson — and I don't typically learn from pleasure.

Don't beat yourself up for making these kinds of mistakes — sometimes you've really got to get into a relationship with someone before their true colors emerge. But when they do, listen to your gut. If you don't feel good about the value system of your so-called friend, it's okay to move on. You don't have to answer to anyone except yourself.

4. **It's called give and take**
   A defining moment in determining whether someone is part of my lady tribe is when things are not so hot. Your mom dies unexpectedly and your inner circle rallies around you by supporting your family in any way possible. Your child's going through a difficult time and you're feeling like a failure, and your friend listens to your worries and fears without judgment. You hate living abroad because you feel lost, and your friend sits with you as you bare your truth.

   These are the deep dives into the abyss of friendship. They're a proving ground for the strength of your bond. It's like your friendship instinct kicks in and you can sense your pal needs your help. Bonds are forged when one of you is at your worst and the other doesn't walk away. If you don't find this happening at either end of the relationship (because you could be the one not pitching in), you might need to step back and reevaluate things.

5. **Just be you**
   I know this is completely cliché, but when you're building a new friendship, don't hide the real you. The goal is to attract the right people — like-minded individuals who make you feel good about who you are. They may not always agree with you, but they'll be willing to tell you that to your face and not behind your back, which is a blinking neon sign of respect.

If you're acting like someone you're not, you'll end up being surrounded by those you can't relate to, and you'll never be able to get past the superficial surface stuff. It might take some time, but when it happens, you'll feel the difference. My real friends don't care if I'm wearing yoga pants to girls' night or if I bring a store-bought cake to Christmas dinner. If they do, that's a clue telling me they may be okay to hang out with on occasion, but they're probably not my people. Okay is a four-letter word too, and it's almost as bad as *fine*. So if you're a swearer, throw an f-bomb into the conversation to see their reaction. If they throw one back, you might be on the right track.

Being an expat and making friends has its challenges, from being on a shortened timeline to having to learn to trust quickly. I mean, there's nothing like asking a total stranger if you can put them down as your child's emergency contact at school. Maybe that person will become someone close to you, but maybe they won't — either way, it's okay. They're figuring out their circle of friends too, and you never know, you might become close later. And if you take them off your emergency contact list... they'll never know.

Find a weirdo just like you and never let them go

The last time I had a 'best friend' was in the sixth grade. I'm not sure what really happened to our friendship; we just grew apart. I assume that's normal, and I don't dwell on it. I felt a bit like a drifter during my teen years, even into college and my early twenties, because I didn't have that one special person who I could trust with my whole heart and knew they felt the same way in return. Maybe I was holding on to a preconceived notion of the ideal best friend. Don't get me wrong, I had friends — great ones that I'm still very close with today. I just never felt like I'd found my person.

As an adult, I no longer feel this way. Now, I have people and lots of best friends. These people are scattered around the world, and I may or may not have heard their voice or seen them in person for months or even years. But when I do, it's like we've never been apart. To me, that's the best thing about true friendship. There's no judgment. It's completely comfortable, and if either of you needs to discuss something that's bothering you, no one's afraid to say it. The best kinds of friendships are easy and don't feel like work.

No longer limiting myself to the idea of having a single best friend makes me feel like the richest person in the world. During my years living abroad, I've grown a global support system of badasses. At any time of the day, one of these women are awake and at the ready. Individually they each serve a different purpose in my life, but together their friendships make me whole. There is nothing like having a badass as a backup. Imagine having an entire army of them.

13

My life is one big IDK

#livinginlimbo

Life status: currently holding it all together with one big bobby pin

Thistle and Wivi are both at sleepovers, so Dandie and Oak decide to grab dinner at their favorite burger joint. It is a parenting *#dreamcometrue*. The couple park themselves at an outdoor table and order drinks. Dandelion feels like Oak's mind is somewhere else. Even though it's Saturday, he went into the office for meetings all day. Dandie noticed a difference in his demeanor when he got home.

"Why'd you have to go in today? Is the sky falling?" asks Dandelion jokingly. She isn't ready for his response.

"Yeah." That's all he says.

Dandelion doesn't understand. "Yeah, what? I need a little more than a one-word answer."

"Well, I don't know how to tell you this…." He's hesitating and it's making Dandelion really uneasy. "They've put our move on hold."

"They what?" spouts Dandelion. "Are you serious?" She immediately loses her appetite and her face slumps in disbelief. A huge bubble of bitterness begins growing inside her – toward those who hold her life in their hands. She wishes Oak had kept the possibility of moving to Switzerland to himself.

"Something happened with the acquisition, and the negotiations have been paused until they can hammer out some major issues. The whole thing seems to be falling apart. It's totally out of my hands."

Oak looks down at his beer and watches the foam dissipate. "I knew you'd be frustrated. I know I am, especially since they've already decided who'll replace me here."

He's right, she feels frustrated. Once you've wrapped your head around the idea of moving, you begin transitioning from one world to another. Now Dandelion's stuck in between worlds.

She can sense disappointment in her husband's voice. He's spoken to her about how excited he is for this opportunity. It's what he's been working so hard for all these years. "Well, bud," she says, "like you said, it's out of our hands. Worrying really isn't going to get us anywhere, so why don't we try to focus on what we can control." [See, you're a good student. The mentee has become the mentor.]

She isn't sure where the calm of those words came from because inside, she is fuming. Expat life is good at throwing curve balls that aren't easy to catch, and this one is full of heat. She's feeling so many different emotions but knows that having a temper tantrum isn't going to make anything better. This isn't her husband's fault, and she knows even though the company isn't always transparent with decision making, they aren't intentionally messing with their lives. They're being hit with corporate shrapnel. Maybe Nietzsche was right, **#whatdoesnotkillyoumakesyoustronger**.

"So now what?" she asks.

"We wait," he replies. He picks at the label on his bottle of beer. "I'm surprised you're taking this so well. I thought you were going to lose your mind." He smiles. "That's why I wanted to break it to you in public."

Dandie laughs. "Oh, believe me, I'd like to lose my mind, but that's not going to change anything. Good plan telling me in public." She swirls her glass of rosé and watches the whirlpool spin inside it. Some days expat life feels like it's spiraling out of control, and this is one of those days. "I think we're still going to move," she says. "I can feel it in my gut."

And Lotus beams with pride.

It's only temporary. All of it.

Each day, Dandie finds herself becoming more and more miffed with having to sit and stew in uncertainty. She's becoming a pest, and she knows it; even she's annoyed with herself. Before Oak can even make it through the door after work, she's harassing him about whether he's heard anything from his company. "Any update?" she's constantly asking even though she promised to let him decompress from work when he got home in the evenings. She sounds like a broken record. And each time, Oak just gets irritated and says, "No, Dand. There's no update. You know I'll tell you the minute I hear something." [Way to know your audience, Dand.]

She doesn't understand how companies can just let people dangle in a sea of ambiguity. For fuck's sake, this is her life last time she checked, but she doesn't feel like she's fully living it because she's waiting for the corner office to make up their mind. *#livinginlimbo* seems to be a dance that so many of her expat pals have become familiar with but are never able to master. No matter how hard she tries to accept the unknown, she can't help from getting irritated.

She knows he isn't trying to be a jerk with his 'this discussion is over' tone, but it still bugs her. How can he be so calm when their life is literally stalled out on the side of the road?

Dandie has a complicated relationship with living in limbo. The simple act of knowing about a possible move switches off her desire to further engage with her current location, and she subconsciously withdraws. Should she make friends with this woman who seems nice? *Nope, I'm probably leaving.* Should she sign up to be a library helper next year? *Uh-uh, I might not be here.*

Even though the idea of moving to Switzerland doesn't have her exactly thrilled, she's curious about the place and can't help herself from embarking on her own personal reconnaissance mission. It's hard for her to really begin to imagine what her new life might look like in Zug, but this doesn't stop her from binge-searching 'life in Switzerland' every night. She obsessively scans the Swiss housing market app on her phone – at least five times a day – endlessly scrolling through houses and apartments that maybe she'll live in one day.

Which neighborhood is the right one to choose? House or apartment? *Definitely house.*

She wishes she could talk to Thistle and Wivi about the possibility of moving. But she doesn't want to plant the idea of leaving in their impressionable young minds too early and turn them into tiny replicas of herself, stuck between two worlds. Letting them live their lives without the burden of knowledge for a little while longer feels like the right choice. Oh, how she wishes she were living in ignorant bliss. Her children are going to be sad to leave a place that has become such a big part of their life. They're no longer little girls who can easily be swayed by talk of new friends and adventure, but they're old enough to know what they're leaving behind, and they aren't going to be pleased about the challenges ahead.

Not being privy to decisions affecting her life is getting to Dandie. It's hard to pretend things are *#normal* when they are clearly *#outofcontrol*.

These days I get most of my exercise from shaking my head in disbelief

"You seem super uptight lately. I assume Oak hasn't heard anything more about moving?" Mags makes her way toward the back patio door that's propped open to let in fresh air. "Where are the plants you're killing and need attention from Aunty Mags?"

"Over there." Dandelion points in the direction of a large grouping of pots that are sitting in a sunny corner of her patio. "And no, we haven't heard anything since he told me he was being transferred." Dandelion fills a watering can with water and brings it over to her friend.

"Did you hear?" says Mags. "Azalea is moving to Korea. She's lucky to be with the US State Department." Mags is happily buzzing from one planter of succulents to another. She always does what she can to prevent Dandelion's plants from knocking on death's door. "I'm kind of jealous of how their expat assignments work." Armed with a watering can and secateurs, Mags keeps her focus on reviving the plants. "I hear they know where they are moving and for how long half a year in advance. Could you imagine knowing where and when you were going to move next?" She pokes fallen leaves back into the soil. "You know you should really do a better job of taking care of these." She glances down at the pots of plump-leaved plants. "We lucked out finding out about our move to Argentina so long ago. It's unheard of, really."

"I know I should," says Dandelion, acknowledging the state of her pathetic parched pots. "And you're right, you knowing where you're moving so far in advance is really unheard of. It'll probably never happen again, so relish the certainty now. Don't forget that one over there." Dandelion points at another pot that needs her friend's attention. "Are you getting excited?"

"About Buenos Aires? I don't know. I guess. I'm just over it." Mags talks to the plants and waters them gently. "It's like, enough already, let's get this shit show on the road."

Dandie notices that Mags is completely checked out. Her mind is already on to her next adventure in Argentina. With one foot out the door, who can blame her for focusing on the future and not the present? She's engrossed in doing all the detailed research work an ASS normally does before arriving in a new destination – she's joined the new expat groups online and has already identified the expat know-it-alls of Buenos Aires.

"The kids have known for ages, and Chestnut is commuting back and forth, so he's permanently jetlagged and grumpy all the time. We're just waiting for the school year to finish. We have the house and the school settled already, the visas are in process, the movers are scheduled, and I've already made plans for the dog to stay here until we get all moved in there."

Dandie wishes she didn't feel twinges of jealousy about her friend's confirmed exit and her detailed plan.

"So," says Mags. "No news on Switzerland yet?"

"Nope." Dandelion stands in the sun with her face to the sky. "I feel like I'm just sitting here wasting time. I'm going to be busting my butt when we finally get some direction."

"Dandie, stop. Stop the woe is me act. I hate to break it to you, but with that kind of attitude, you'll be busting your butt harder than necessary. You know exactly what you need to do. Stop acting so naïve and helpless. You've done this before, and you know better." Magnolia talks to Dandelion like a big sister, and she isn't afraid to give her a swift kick in the rump when she needs it.

"Alright, simmer down. I hear you." Dandelion knows she's right.

My life is kind of like when you're about to sneeze and then don't

Dandelion hits the call button on the computer and a second later Sunflower's face pops up on the screen. "Hi."

Not knowing the call has connected, Sunflower is startled by Dandelion's voice. "Oh, shoot. Hey." She looks like she's still getting herself together for their session. "You caught me in the middle of putting on my face." She has a tube of lipstick in one hand and a small compact mirror in the other. She finishes coating her lips with the dark pink paint and clicks the mirror shut. "Okay. I'm ready."

"Everything okay? I didn't mean to rush you. Do you need a few minutes?" asks the client. Dandelion notices a difference in Sunflower's energy. She's not her usual perky self.

"Nah. I'm good." She waves a hand at the screen. "Just a case of the Tuesdays." She pours herself a tall glass of water and immediately drains it. "You know what it's like to juggle too many things at once. My husband's been traveling on business for the past couple of weeks and this mama is exhausted." She pats her mouth dry with a tissue and then presses it on her cheeks and forehead. Sunflower isn't ashamed of admitting she's knackered and doing so seems to lift her spirit a little. The woman is *#keepingitreal*.

"Preach it, sister," Dandelion replies. She knows exactly how the woman feels, so it's easy to empathize with her. *Even the ones who always seem to have their shit together have hard days.*

"So, tell me what's going on in your world," asks Sunflower.

That's Dandelion's cue to clue her coach in on all the remarkable breakthroughs she's been making. But there aren't any. Instead of trying to keep moving forward, Dandelion has opted for the status quo. All this talk of transition and living in limbo makes her feel like she's backpedaling a bit when it comes to her own metamorphosis. Treading water is all she can do to keep herself from going nuts.

"I hate living in limbo. Our move to Switzerland is on hold and may not happen." Dandelion spits the words out with disgust. "I'm just so fucking frustrated."

"Tell me how you really feel," chortles Sunflower. "At least you're able to name your emotions."

Dandelion laughs at her sounding board's reaction. It's true. She's not one for holding back when it comes to voicing her frustrations. "I just hate living in between worlds – living in a place you can no longer give your whole heart to, while beginning a journey to a new one with no definitive timeline on the horizon. It's like a total false start." She knows Sunflower will understand this comment, like any fellow expat. "It's expat purgatory."

Sunflower responds swiftly. "Okay. So, you are literally stuck between a rock and a hard place. What are you going to do about it?"

"I hate it when you make me fix my own problems." Dandelion leans back in her chair and lets her head hang loose in defeat. "Well, according to my friend Mags, I need to take control of the things in my life that I'm actually able to control."

"Your friend is very wise. She's made my job very easy today because I would've told you the exact same thing."

"Don't tell her that, I don't want her to get a big head," Dandelion jokes. "I know she's right. It's just easier to wallow in self-pity." This double reality check makes Dandelion realize she needs to slap herself out of expat purgatory and start living in the moment again. Living for the 'what ifs' of life is too damn exhausting.

"Dandelion, you don't want pity. I know you. You want action." Sunflower isn't looking at her but typing something into a document. "So what actions are you going to put into motion?"

Dandelion rattles off the list of things she and Mags discussed and knows she's going to be told to get off her ass and start doing them. She decides to preempt being told off. "I'll start prepping for this move tomorrow. I promise. I'm going to be ready when they get things ironed out. I know it's going to happen. I can feel it in my gut."

Lotus sits happily in the comfort of being seen.

"Good," says Sunflower. "Then I won't need to use my angry mom voice with you." Sunny seems to be in a better mood as they are ending their session. Her tone is much more jovial. "You know what to do, Dandelion. Be like Nike, and just do it."

Dandelion takes the advice of her friend and coach. She pulls up her bootstraps and steps out of the vortex of pity. If she wants to feel like she has any power over her life, it's up to her to create that control.

She sends in the school application forms and requests total anonymity. *Please do not share my information with any parents at this time,* she writes to the admissions department upon receiving the acceptance letter – the last thing she wants is a welcome email or invitation to be sent to an online group where she may know other expats from Oak's company. She hates company politics.

She clears out every closet in the house and donates 15 bags of clothes. Next, she works her way through the playroom, where she organizes, tosses, and donates the girls' toys, books, and craft supplies. She cleans out the medicine cabinets, trashes old pool toys, and goes through the filing cabinet. She sells outgrown bikes and scooters collecting dust in the garage, unloads furniture she doesn't love anymore, and pares down her holiday decoration collection by half. And she gathers all the documents the immigration service provider will require – apostilled versions of birth and marriage certificates, updated passports, and vaccine records.

When Oak comes home to tell her his transfer is back on, she'll be ready. Packing her life into a container will be like finishing a jigsaw puzzle, each piece fitting perfectly into place. She'll be completely prepared for all the surprises that come along with an international move. Yeah, yeah; who is she trying to kid?

I'm too busy working on my own grass to notice if yours is greener

The PTA needs to find fresh meat for next year's slate of suckers. The current members begin milling about finding out who's in, who's out, and who's on the fence at the beginning of the second term of school. Dandelion has no interest in being in, and moving to Switzerland is helping squash the pangs of guilt that she can't help feeling.

Dandelion walks out of the elementary school office after dropping Wivi and Thistle off late. They had early morning dentist appointments, and she had to sign them in with the school secretary. Before heading home, she stops at the parent lounge to grab a coffee. She needs an extra caffeine jolt after forgetting her travel mug this morning.

A coffee morning or parent talk is wrapping up, and the lounge is packed with faces. She makes her way over to the snack-shop counter and orders a to-go coffee.

"Hey, Dandie, we were just talking about you. Were your ears bleeding?" A couple of Chatty Cactuses wave her over.

Dandelion pays for her coffee, grabs the to-go cup, and walks over to the ladies. "Hello. I hope you were only saying good things." She snickers.

"We are planning next year's event coordinators, and we wanted to make sure you'd plan the Welcome Back Coffee like this year. You did such a great job," says one of Petunia's Cactuses, throwing her a compliment.

Dandelion hasn't prepared herself for questions about future events and doesn't have a good response ready. She takes a sip from her steamy cup to stall. "Ugh," she stammers, trying to think quickly on her feet, "it shouldn't be a problem." *I mean, it could be if I'm not actually here to help.* She can't look the woman in the eye. "I think it would be good if there was someone co-chairing the event with me. Can you try to find someone?" Dandelion knows that having a co-chair means they'll be someone to pick up the pieces she leaves behind. Don't forget to **#coveryourass**.

"I saw you were selling a bunch of your stuff on the local expat group. Are you moving?" inquires one of the Cactuses. "I wish I'd known you were going to sell that wine cabinet. It was stunning."

"Oh, yeah. I saw that too," the other Cactus interjects. "You've gotta tell us when you're selling something good."

Across the room, PTA Petunia sees the Cactuses and Dandelion chatting and immediately turns her well-tuned ear in their direction. The Cactuses aren't being nosey, but Petunia certainly is.

Dandelion notices Petunia from the corner of her eye. "Um, no. I, ugh, just can't stand clutter. I figure why hold on to things you don't love or aren't using?" She's fumbling over her own tongue. "It was nice seeing you, ladies. I'm sorry, but I've got to run." Dandelion gets the hell out of there as fast as she can. Of course it looks like she's purging before a move, but who really cares about what she is doing?

Dandelion assumes that PTA Petunia, ever the one to have her ear glued to someone else's conversation, sniffs a rat. Dandie had been super vague and noncommittal with the Cactuses, and what if Petunia had heard her ask for a co-chair? Everyone knows Dandie's capable of doing that job with one hand tied behind her back. *Maybe Petunia didn't hear*, hopes the limbo queen. But she's sure Petunia also saw her selling that furniture.

When Dandelion gets into the safety of her car, she takes a deep breath. She thought she'd been so sly about her downsizing, but it's obvious she's being obvious. *Let them make assumptions. I really don't care.*

#MYTHEORY

My first experience with expat life was a real doozy. One year before my husband and I moved to Geneva in 2009, we were set to move to Prague. We'd made two trips to the Czech Republic and found a home to live in, a pre-school for our daughter, applied for our visas, and scheduled the movers. Three weeks before the movers were to pack our container and send it across the ocean, my husband's company canceled our move to Prague and told us we would still be moving but they didn't know where. I had quit my job, pulled our daughter out of daycare, and mentally prepared myself and our entire family for our departure. My whole life had been modified for this new adventure.

For nine months, I lived in limbo. Looking back, I struggled with commitment, identity woes, and resentment for the entire expat process. I was over it before it even began. I didn't know how to move forward and create a life because I'd never experienced this in-between space, nor did I know anyone else who'd lived it. Five international moves later and a shipping container of badass experience, I wish I could go back and hand myself this book — so I'd know what I was experiencing was a real thing.

I don't know where I'm going, but I'm on my way

Nothing can be done when living through periods of uncertainty except to be patient. I know that sounds easier said than done, but worrying certainly isn't going to help the situation. A foolproof plan can still get hijacked by something completely out of our control — military coups (yes, I know people who have fled their host country), visa issues, medical problems, or a job opportunity that's fallen through.

Having experienced this weird 'in-between' several times, I've learned a few ways to work around feeling like my life is on hold and I'm waiting for customer service to finally take my call. In effect, I put on the speakerphone and start emptying the dishwasher.

1. **Take control**
   A great way for me to tame unwanted anxiety is to harness control of what's within my reach. I get my house in order, metaphorically and literally. I stop putting off all the things I've been meaning to do, from making sure the kids are up to date with their health checks to cleaning out the closets and organizing the important documents I'll inevitably be asked for down the road. It's like doing a massive spring clean of my life. Why ruin today stressing about things

outside of my control? Instead, I'd rather be productive. I might not be able to schedule the movers yet, but I'll be ready when I can.

2. **Be present**

    I know you don't want to hear it, but pushing yourself to live in the present will make you happier. Allowing myself to live in the moment set me free from the perpetual feeling of being suspended between heaven and hell. It helped me focus on being grateful for all the good in my life and stopped me from wasting the time I had left, wherever I was in the world. It's about making the most of the precious time I have with my friends, experiencing the world with my family, and taking full advantage of the expat adventure. So, plan that bucket-list trip you've been wanting to take and buy the travel insurance — you'll be sad if you miss out on making it a reality. I didn't always do this, and I have some regrets, but I now know the weight of letting those things slip through my fingers and I'm not willing to chance that again.

3. **Embrace flexibility**

    I know I'm driving this point home pretty hard, but I think it's important. Schedules and plans are amazing, but life doesn't go according to a minute-by-minute itinerary. So I've learned to live in a more fluid state. And by this I mean having a mindset that can shift when needed — and without resistance, resentment, or regret weighing you down. Imagine you're in a maze, and you've hit a dead end. What are you going to do? Keep banging on the wall hoping it'll miraculously open? I doubt it. You'd most likely double back, regroup, and look for a new route. Living in limbo is like that. Don't miss out on living by allowing roadblocks to get in your way — find another path and keep going.

Once I shifted my perspective, I had an easier time dealing with the unknown. Of course, there was still uncertainty in my life, but it wasn't the driving force.

When someone asks where you see yourself in 10 years: "Buddy, I'm just trying to make it to Friday."

I am a planner. I like preparing for parties, vacations, and even my week ahead. In a former life, I was a master production scheduler for a large manufacturing facility. People used to pay me to craft a plan – it was the perfect job for me. I planned and replanned until I thought it was perfect. Life was good until it wasn't – little hiccups would be resolvable, but major shutdowns would create moments of inactivity, lost productivity, and lost sales. When things went wrong, people would get panicky, start micromanaging the situation, and begin brainstorming 'what if' scenarios.

These glitches brought the worst out in me because they voided my perfectly laid out plan and took away my control. Once things were close to being back up and running, I would reevaluate and regain control by managing within my limitations. Little by little, the limitations would shrink and eventually I'd be back planning an optimal schedule.

Over time, I learned to make my production plans as malleable as possible, always keeping my focus on what was controllable. New issues were constantly cropping up. I couldn't control every outcome; production runs were sometimes short, maybe I'd transpose a number, or the crew would just do the wrong thing. It was the nature of the beast and I had to roll with the punches.

I think this life experience helped me survive numerous episodes of expat limbo because it basically taught me that shit will always happen. Being connected to a cryptic future is difficult. You've got multiple scenarios playing out in your head — most of which won't come true — and this makes you irrational and drains your energy. You can either wallow in the uncertainty or you can pivot and move on. I choose to move on.

14

Your work is not your worth

#purpose

Écoute-moi (Listen to me)

Dandelion is feeling conflicted with all the ups and downs of living abroad. Even though she embraces a life that is unpredictable, she's troubled with the suspense of living in limbo again. She's overwhelmed, but this time she knows it and has the tools to deal with it properly. Combatting these emotions doesn't come naturally, but she's trying her damndest.

Stepping into the shower after an intense boxing session, Dandelion feels drained. She stands under the hot water as it falls onto her head and shoulders and winces as her body adjusts to the temperature. The water is a bit too hot, but Dandie resists turning the cold-water knob because the heat is softening the tension in her neck. She lowers her head forward and lets the water pulse the back of her body like a masseuse. She relaxes and begins to sob.

All the emotional *#baggage* she's been carrying around falls to the shower's tiled floor and bursts open like an overstuffed suitcase. The bittersweet release is long overdue; every day, Dandie's been putting on her big girl pants to keep her crazy train from going off the rails. At least her adult temper tantrum is hidden from the real world behind steamy walls of tempered glass.

She's been working her tail off continuing to balance her family's life while figuring out how to live in the moment. Steadying herself to say goodbye to a place she has come to love is emotionally and physically difficult. Even though she is trying her best not to live in a 'woe is me' state of mind, she has her moments. She has so much on her mind and is worried about Oak's outlook on the future. These hiccups are not signs of weakness, rather the raw realness of life reminding her she isn't *#bulletproof*. The shrapnel of expat life can tear a hole in your armor without any warning.

"I'm so fucking tired," bawls Dandelion. "I'm so fucking over it. No one tells you about the emotional mind fuck of being an expat when you sign on the dotted line. I don't want to move again. But I have no choice because I don't belong here. I never have a choice." She squirts shampoo into her palm and rubs her hands together vigorously before starting to work the suds into her scalp. "I never have a fucking choice." She isn't even really sure what she's upset about anymore, but freeing the pent-up emotions is cathartic.

Ten minutes later, she turns off the taps and takes a moment to pull herself together with one last deep breath. Dandie's all cried out for today. Patting her face dry, she looks straight in the eyes of her mirrored reflection and growls, "Stop fucking worrying about stuff you can't control."

"We're trying, but it's hard," says a voice in her head. Lotus is trying to show Dandelion how hard they've been working.

"It is, but crying isn't going to change anything," says Dandelion, rebuking her own intuition.

"You're right, it won't. But we can't always hush our emotions. We need a good cry once in a while, so deal with it." Lotus is on a rampage and Dandelion knows her little friend is right. There's no reason to feel shame or deny herself the feelings of frustration, annoyance, and resentment. "We're going to do what's best for us," Lotus continues. "So who's the *#badass* now? We haven't been working this hard over the past nine months for you to start acting like a helpless *#flailingspouse* who doesn't know who she is or what she wants. It's time for you to *#suckitupsister* because we still have lots of work ahead of us."

Staring at her twin image, Dandelion is stunned from the asswhooping her gut just handed her. She attempts a rebuttal but is cut off by Lotus before she can get the first syllable out of her mouth.

"Don't let us down, Dandelion. We deserve all the feels. We deserve fulfillment and happiness. We deserve something more than what we've settled for all these years when we were making here and there our home." Lotus is getting emotional. "Now is our chance to redefine what that is to us. WE are not them; WE go by the beat of our own drummer. To hell with finding purpose – let's just live life to the fullest and see where it takes us."

Dandelion closes her eyes and accepts Lotus' challenge. "Okay. Let's do this." Lotus' request is simple and isn't rigid with rules. It's sincere and organic by design. They are fully in sync, and together they are ready to be the badass they were always meant to be.

Living on the brink of another life transition just might be the best space in time for this learning process to come full circle. Technically, it has nothing to do with where she physically lives; the knowledge resides within and will follow her wherever life takes her. Like the fluffy white seeds of a fully-bloomed dandelion, she is ready – with confidence – to take root wherever the wind may take her.

It feels good to be lost in the right direction

Dandelion is a bit jumpy about her next session with Sunflower. She texted Dandelion earlier in the week to say she'd like to discuss core values and purpose. She also asked Dandelion to brainstorm what she thinks this phase of her journey will uncover for her. Dandelion's first thought after reading the text was, *WTF is this?*

Sitting at her desk with a pen and blank notebook, Dandelion writes the word *PURPOSE* at the top of the page. The sight of that word makes her recoil, and she thinks back to the conversation she had with Lotus in the mirror. "I don't like this word," she mutters. She rips the page from her notebook and tosses it into the trash. "I've got to look at this differently."

Dandelion struggles to come up with a replacement word for purpose. Not wanting to feel like she's wasting time, she scribbles the word 'future' in the center of the page and circles it. Next, she writes: *community, family, writing, honesty*. She fills the entire page with words – *blogging, friendship, happiness, health, creativity, Switzerland, transition, moving, helping, expression, authenticity, confidence* – the list goes on and on. Her recent homework assignment helps put into words the fundamentals of what makes Dandie who she is today.

Once she finishes her free-thinking session, Dandie sits back to review what she's produced. She doesn't have much to say about it. *Just looks like a bunch of nonsense to me.* She looks down at the black dog curled up like a cinnamon roll beside her, his glassy eyes glancing up at her. "What do you think?" She opens her desk drawer, takes out a rainbow of colored pens, and begins categorizing the words, circling them with different colors. After a few moments, she begins to see four main areas emerge: words circled in red are about connection, the ones in blue are about imagination, the green ones are about helping, and the yellows are about sense of self.

Unknowingly, she's determining what's important to her wellbeing – her core values: Genuineness, Creativity, Usefulness, and Humility.

Sunflower quizzes her. "Did you do your homework?"

"Yes, though I had a hell of a time with it at first," says Dandelion.

"That's pretty normal." Sunflower looks to be searching her computer for something. "Did you send it to me?"

"I uploaded a picture." Dandelion is flipping through her notebook looking for the homework and lifts up the notebook to show the screen when she finds the page. "It looks like this."

"Got it." Sunflower double-clicks the file, and a very colorful diagram pops up on her screen. "Wow."

Feeling like her homework looks a little childlike, Dandelion says, "I know. It's a disaster."

"Stop. It's great. What does it mean?" asks Sunflower.

"Isn't that what I'm paying *you* for?" Dandie snorts. She smiles, pulls her notebook closer, and begins to walk her coach through the spiderweb of thoughts.

When her client is done, Sunflower takes a minute to look it over. "So, you've identified four main areas that seem to be your core values, right?"

"I guess."

"I'm not surprised with your answers, but I'd like to get a bit deeper with them. Why is creativity so important to you?"

Dandie tries to explain. "I don't know. I never really thought I was an artist, but I've always done some sort of art. I was a dancer growing up, and I love writing. People seem to think I'm pretty good at it."

"Agreed. So tell me more. Is it a passion?"

"Well, yeah. I guess. Whenever I start thinking about what I enjoy doing, I seem to come back to writing. I'm guessing it means I want my future to include it in some way."

"That's awesome."

"I suppose." Dandelion sloughs off the compliment because she isn't comfortable with the idea of being a real writer.

"Say, 'I'm a writer,'" demands the sunny disposition staring back at her.

"But I'm not a writer."

"Say it."

"No."

"Say it."

"I'm a writer."

"Do you believe it?"

"Nope."

"Okay, you will. We'll work on that some more later. Let's keep going." Sunflower scans the document and says, "You've circled the word 'usefulness.' Which is ironic because I know you have an aversion to the word 'purpose.'"

Dandelion is looking down and scanning the document. "To me, usefulness isn't purpose – it's adding value." She looks down at the notebook again. "It seems I like to help people."

"That's a good characteristic. How do you turn that into something?" probed Sunflower.

"Why do I have to turn it into something?" Dandelion isn't liking the idea of turning her tendency to help others into a 'something.'

"I mean, I guess you don't." Sunflower looks perplexed. "Do you want to try to create something you will eventually be able to monetize?"

"I'm not doing this for money or other people." She holds up the color-splattered paper. "I am doing this for me."

"I hear you, but I'm just wondering if you see the potential in yourself that I see in you." It's as if Sunflower is trying to slowly back away from a lion that's ready to pounce but lays a trap before she hides. "I think you've got the expert knowledge to help other women who are just like you."

"Packing up your life and moving it to another country every few years doesn't exactly make me an expert at anything."

"You're fucking kidding, right? You don't think you're an expert expat?"

Dandelion secretly loves it when her coach speaks to her like a peer and not a client. "I'm not an expert at anything." [Your husband thinks you're an expert at being a pain in the ass.]

"I hate to break it to you, but yes, you are an expert. You've been the maestro of moving your family from one continent to another for the past decade. Do you know how daunting that is for some individuals? I bet people would pay good money to get advice from someone with experience like you. I'm not going to go any further with this because I can see you're not feeling it right now. Just promise me you won't rule it out."

"Alright. But that's not my focus right now." [***#neversaynever***, Dandelion.]

"This is great work, Dandie. I'm super proud of you." Sunflower is smiling from ear to ear. "Keep this going. Now, I want you to envision your future."

Later that night, nursing a hot ginger tea, Dandelion replays her conversation with Sunflower over and over. Is she selling herself short? She doesn't think so. Dandelion is certain she isn't looking for a career – at least not at this point in her life. *I just want to be me: the girl who goes by the beat of her own drummer, a genuine person who enjoys writing and lending a helping hand – if it's on her own terms.*

The past decade of her life has been a rollercoaster of constant adjustment. She seems to have done a decent job riding the wave, but the past nine months working with Sunflower have launched her into a new realm of personal enlightenment. She knows her purpose is driven by fulfillment and happiness, not dollar signs. And she's discovering the elements that manifest those things in her life – Genuineness, Creativity, Usefulness, and Humility. But what does it look like?

She heads to her office and grabs a basket of old magazines, a piece of blank white paper, scissors, a glue stick, and some magic markers. In big bold letters she writes each of her core values on the sheet of paper. She grabs a stack of magazines, rips pages from the spines, and looks for phrases and words that will help create her vision, pictures of people, and places.

Like an elementary-school student, she cuts them up and glues them on the page, mish-mashed like an overlapping collage of thought and concept. The vision board is covered in bold expressions like 'Your comeback starts here' and 'Watch me move on with a smile.' She's glued on a picture of her favorite outfit – a white-collared shirt and jeans – which signifies her sense of knowing herself and what makes her feel confident. There are pink boxing gloves representing femininity and strength, and lots of flowers reminding her to never give up blooming. When she's done, she looks up at the bulletin board hanging next to her desk. It's full of kitschy mementos – silent reminders of the past.

"I have a wonderful past, but this is for the future," she says as she tacks her collage to the bulletin board, covering photos of smiling faces, ticket stubs, and notes. The souvenirs of the past are not to be forgotten; she is lovingly setting them aside to make way for the new version of Dandelion. They will always be part of her, just maybe not at the forefront of who she is today. Today's version of Dandelion isn't the same as tomorrow's.

I want Felicia's life. She's always going somewhere.

Pacing up and down the aisles of the grocery store, Dandelion plucks things off the shelves to make dinner. It's getting cooler every day, and that morning her girls had asked if she'd make chicken noodle soup for dinner. *I'll make anything if you'll actually eat it*, she'd said to herself.

As she grabs a bag of wavy egg noodles from the shelf, her phone vibrates in her purse. She rummages through the bottomless pit of a bag, but by the time she finds the phone, it's stopped ringing. *Missed call from Oak. Wonder what he wants.* Her husband rarely calls her during the day. *If it's important, he'll text me.* She plops the phone back in her bag and continues down the grocery store aisle. A minute later it buzzes again and she takes the call. "Hello."

"Hey, Dand. Where are you?" asks her husband.

It's two o'clock in the afternoon on a Tuesday; where else would she be? "I'm at the grocery store."

The signal is shaky inside the store and Oak's response is cutting out. "Can you—copies—passports?"

"What? Hold on a sec. I need to find a better signal."

He says something in response but it's inaudible. She walks toward the entrance of the store and his voice becomes crystal clear.

"Okay," she says. "Sorry, what did you say again?" This better be good because she's almost done with her shopping.

"I said, can you send me copies of our passports?"

"Yes, when I get home." She's sounding annoyed. She hates it when he makes her feel like his assistant.

"When will that be?" he counters.

"I don't know. I'm out running errands. Is it *that* important?"

"Kind of – if we plan to move to Switzerland. I need to send copies to the immigration lawyers today. The company's completed their negotiations, and our move is back on. They want me there as soon as possible. We can finally let the cat out of the bag."

Of course they fucking want you there as soon as possible.

"Dand? You still there?" Oak's sounding rushed. "I've gotta run into a meeting. We can talk about all this later. Send me the passports when you get home."

"Yeah. Okay—"

The phone goes click.

Oak's phone call has shaken Dandie. She just went from living in limbo to another international move. She can't tell if she's happy, sad, relieved, or annoyed. She's been waiting for this decision for three months, and now it has finally been revealed like a jack-in-the-box – you know it's coming but you're still not ready for it to pop out at you.

In 10-plus years of living abroad, Dandie has been uprooted and moved around the world several times – from Switzerland and Belgium to Mexico and South Africa. With each relocation, her expat life became as normal as it can be when you're living in a place that's beyond foreign. But somehow, each location became a precious piece of her that was so familiar she could not imagine living without it. It's everything she loves about expat life – the learning, the cultures, the people, the adventure – and everything she hates.

Dandelion chats to the cashiers as she puts her groceries on the conveyor belt to pay, then makes her way toward the parking lot. A young porter approaches her. The name 'Mopane' is embroidered on his smock. "Hello, mum. May I help you with your groceries?" he asks. He takes her shopping cart from her before she can respond. "How is your day going?"

"Um. It's pretty good, Mopane." [Is it good?] "How is yours?"

"The sun is shining and I'm still breathing, so it can't be a bad day," he replies. His smile is big and bright, and he's got swagger. After he puts the last bag of groceries into the boot of Dandelion's car, he hits the button to close the hatch and turns to look at her. "I can't wait for tomorrow because the memory of today will be a reminder of who I used to be. You know, you always have to be changing."

"You do? Why?" She hands him a tip for helping her.

"Yo. You know you gotta be ready for what life hands you, mum. The good and the bad."

Dandelion is surprised by this young guy's view. She wonders if he's dealt with a lot of ups and downs in his short life. Maybe it hasn't been very easy. "Well, Mopane," she says, "I admire your outlook."

He puts the money in his pocket and looks at her. "We only get one chance, so we gotta be willing to give it all we got. Have a good day, mum. *Sharp-sharp.*" He smiles again, turns, and trots over to another woman exiting the shopping center with a full cart of groceries.

Dandelion gets in her car and watches the porter for another minute or so. He's hustling and smiling at the same time. *You always have to be changing*, she says to herself. In a weird way, his words validate her reimagined idea of purpose: she can be this version of Dandelion today and another tomorrow.

Nobody tests your inner gangster more than your daughter's smart mouth

"Hey girls," says Oak, "we need to talk to you. Can you come outside?"

The family convenes around the patio table. It's quiet, and all you can hear is the automatic pool cleaner bubbling in the black-bottom pool and a go-away-bird cawing in a nearby tree, its call actually sounding like it's crying "go away." *Oh*, Dandelion says to herself, *we're going away alright*.

"So, girls, we have some big news." Oak pauses for a moment. "We're moving to Switzerland!" He's waiting for some sort of reaction out of them.

"Well, duh. We know," says Wivi without looking at either of them. She pulls a wad of chewing gum out of her mouth and examines it.

"Huh?" her parents say in unison, looking at each other in disbelief.

"Put your gum back in your mouth," Oak orders. "That's gross."

Wivi looks over at him and mischievously pops the wad of gum back in her mouth.

Dandelion intervenes. "How'd you know we were moving?"

"You guys aren't very good at keeping secrets, Mom," says Thistle. "We" – she looks over at her sister – "may speak two languages, but one of them is English. We understand what you and Dad talk about in hushed voices. We aren't deaf."

These are the moments when Dandelion wishes she and her husband spoke a secret language.

Oak looks over at Dandie, and she can't help but laugh.

"Okay," says Oak, "so what do you think?"

"I don't want to move," says Thistle. "I like it here. I like my friends and I love my horse."

"You'll make new friends and I know they have horses there," tries Dandie, knowing her defense is weak but not having much else to offer. *I like my life too.*

"Yeah, but I don't *want* to make new friends or ride other horses." Thistle's comeback is extra prickly.

"Me neither," agrees Wivi. "I like it here." She's pulling her gum like taffy between her fingers and teeth.

Their mother's heart sinks. Their reaction confirms this won't be one of those moves where the promise of great things makes it all better. They're not babies, they're miniature globetrotters who've moved more times in their short lives than Dandelion and Oak had moved in their first 30 years of life. They may be seasoned at moving, but they're still kids.

"I know this is hard, girls," acknowledges Oak, "but we've always known living here would be temporary. My job is changing, and we have no choice but to move to Switzerland."

"We know," says Thistle. "It doesn't mean we have to like it, though."

You and me both, kid, thinks Dandie.

"Do you promise we can come back and visit?" asks Wivi. "I want to visit my horse."

"Absolutely. You have my word," Oak assures them.

It's a promise Dandelion knows he will keep because she's keenly aware of how much he, too, is drawn to South Africa.

"So," says Oak, "how about we come back for Christmas next year?"

I'm jealous of the people who get to see you every day

"I just thought you would be moving home," says Dandelion's mom on the video call. Her eyes look sad. "I'm sure you're excited, though." She forces a smile.

Dandelion appreciates the effort but knows how upset the news of her family staying overseas makes her mom feel. This is a conversation she's had with her parents five times, and it never gets easier.

"You know we'll probably never move *home*." Dandelion's a little irritated by her mother's statement but is trying her best not to sound it. She isn't sure what the right words to say are, so she apologizes. "I'm sorry, Mom."

"You know what I meant – back to the US." Her mother wipes away a tear before it can ruin her rouge-stained cheeks. "I just wish we got to see you and the girls more."

Dandelion tries to make their upcoming move sound like an improvement. "We'll only be one ten-hour flight away. So at least we'll be a bit closer." She slaps a big grin on her face in hopes of making her mom smile.

"Honey, you know your mom and I just miss you," her dad chimes in.

Her parents are sitting on the sofa with the phone in front of them, but all Dandelion can see is half of each face and most of their nasal cavities.

"I know, Dad."

"We are very proud of you. We raised a very brave and independent daughter." Dandie's dad looks over at her mom. "Didn't we?"

"Yes. It must be hard to keep moving to all these new places – starting all over again and again."

Mom, you have no idea. "Thanks," says Dandelion. She's lucky to have parents who are so proud and supportive of the choices she's made in life. But she can't stop feeling guilty for all the years they've missed out on being around her and Oak and the girls – all because they've been living abroad.

"Tell Oak we said congratulations," says her mom. "And give the girls a kiss from us. We have to get going."

"Okay, I will. Where are you headed off to?" Dandelion is astonished that her parents are done with the conversation so quickly.

"We're meeting our friends at the coffee shop," her mom replies. "At least we have some new news to offer up to today's discussion." Dandelion can tell they're walking now because she's getting a nice shot of the ceiling fan. "We'll talk to you later, honey."

Dandie smiles. "Glad I could offer up some interesting conversation topics for you and your friends." She's imagining what kind of stories her father will tell over weak coffee and bagels. "I'll call you next week."

"Love you, honey," they both say before hanging up, and even though their phone etiquette is questionable, it makes their daughter laugh.

"Love you too," says Dandie. But she's talking to a dark screen.

A new image of Dandelion is taking shape. It's still rough around the edges and missing puzzle pieces, but the picture is coming into a hazy focus. It's not quite the life she had envisioned. Instead, the Alps are flanking her, cows are grazing around every corner, and cheese takes center stage. But hey, that's expat life.

She's ready to tackle the unexpected twists and turns her journey will be sure to throw at her. Her resolve to live intentionally accompanied by her laser focus in making *something* a thing of the past confirms she's no longer just *fine*. A single purpose will not define her, but a life full of wonder and worth will. Dandelion's a bona fide *badass abroad*.

#MYTHEORY

One night riding home in the back of an Uber van, a very intoxicated friend quietly slurred, "It's like it's me, but it's not me." At the time, I nearly peed my pants from laughing so hard. But once I'd sobered up, I found the words quite thought-provoking. If I compare an older version of myself with the current one, I can say the same — it's like it's me, but it's not me... anymore.

When I look back and think about my identity revolution, figuring out what I wanted out of life wasn't an 'a-ha' moment. I'd describe it as a collection of learnings that ended up helping me define a clearer path to intentional living. I don't just have one reason for existing; I have many. Some overlap, some don't. But they're all things I deliberately try to achieve with the moxie that's always existed in my soul.

Your soul is rooting for you

The word 'purpose' feels a bit played out and permanent. Instead, I like the notion of an ever-evolving force that propels me to pursue an even better version of myself day after day, all the while filling my soul with satisfaction. It's like I'm always moving in a forward motion — changing, learning, and developing new thoughts and ideas — but the speed varies from warp speed to a snail's pace. That constant momentum keeps me untethered from a plan that may become *passé* during my time on this planet.

I had to (re)define some things before I was able to decipher the secret code of my *purpose*. I'm not a fan of the word or even the idea of purpose — instead, I like to refer to it as objective nirvana. The definition of objective is something toward which effort is directed, and nirvana is a goal hoped for but apparently unattainable. So if I'm always trying to push my energy toward a goal that's pretty hard to achieve, I'll always be pushing for an advancement of self.

I'm drawn to the idea of objective nirvana because the ultimate thing I want out of life is happiness and fulfillment, which is hard as hell to achieve all the time. I also try to make sure I keep my objective nirvana flexible because what brings me happiness and fulfillment today might not bring it to me later.

I think there are three key fundamentals when it comes to creating objective nirvana – *values, vision,* and *passion.* These, too, are in constant motion. I'm certain these things have transformed over the span of my life, and they'll continue to do so till the day I die. Let's face it, the reason I no longer enjoy the sweet taste of White Zinfandel is that my palate has come a long way from that 22-year-old trying to look like a real adult. These days, I'm drinking dry rosé like a boss.

1. **Determine your values**
   Values are the beliefs that guide the way you live your life. They are important to your wellbeing. Everyone has a unique set of values, and these core traits determine the direction our lives will take us. You'll most likely be drawn to people who have similar values as you. Maybe that's why you feel an immediate connection to certain people.

   You can find countless lists of core values on the internet. Print one out and whittle it down until you have a top-10 list, then whittle it down some more. Sculpt a shortlist of words that encompass the basics of your wellbeing. This list may change over time as your priorities shift through different phases of your life. I think it's a good idea to check in with your values on occasion because values help us live our most authentic life, and a little adjustment to our values can make a big impact on our existence.

2. **Ignite your vision**
   Vision is the image you manifest about your future. This is a fun way to dream about what you want your life to look and feel like. Sit back and really think about what you want – visualize it until you can almost taste it.

I enjoy using vision boards when crafting the optics of a future version of myself. It's a creative way to help me home in on what I'm trying to achieve or change. I keep them simple and small enough for me to pin up within eyesight as little reminders of what I'm trying to accomplish. Over time, your vision might get more complex, but that's because you'll build it bigger each time you achieve your goals. Your vision is yours alone. Put on blinders and keep looking forward; don't compare yourself to others. You don't want what *they* want, you want what *you* want.

3. **Chase your passions**
   Passion is the intense desire felt by a person for something. Our passions are what fuel our internal joy and fill our souls, and I believe it's essential to make these elements part of our daily lives.

   My passions vary from writing to pushing my physical limits (within reason), and I try to give them each the attention they deserve. For instance, I love to ski, and I carve time out of my busy life to fulfill that passion by hitting the slopes to feel the freeness of gliding down the mountain. Sometimes I fall, but I get back up, have a good laugh at myself, and dust off the snow before taking off again. Having passion isn't about doing something perfectly; it's about doing what makes you happy no matter what.

Going through the process of defining my objective nirvana was an eye-opening experience. It uncovered some things that surprised me (like how much I value creativity in my life), but it also confirmed what I already believed to be true (my high regard for genuineness).

I'm aware that I am rare

My mother-in-law likes to tell the story of me and my husband's first wedding anniversary. She'd called to wish us a happy anniversary, and while chatting with her, my husband said, "It's been a great year. No big fights." Her response was, "Well, that's because you always know where you stand with Claire." That was 19 years ago. Maybe some values don't change; I guess I've always been living a life of genuineness.

Be honest with yourself and listen to your heart when you redesign your purpose. Like me, you might call it something else, and your idea of what it looks like will probably be completely different too. Just like snowflakes, each one of us is different – we all have different values, visions, and passions. This is what makes each of us unique. Being vulnerable to the process can open ourselves up to new opportunities for growth and development in ways we never thought possible. I know it did for me, and I bet it will for you too. We've just got to be brave enough to embrace the challenge of change.

15

Your new life is going to cost you your old one

#badass

That's a horrible idea. What time?

Dandelion's cleaning the kitchen when she hears the front door open. She looks up to see Oak rounding the corner. He looks wiped out. Their eyes meet as he dumps his briefcase on the counter. Fourteen hours earlier the couple stood in the same spot looking crisp and ready to take on the day ahead of them.

"Hey, buddy," Dandelion says to greet her husband. "You hungry?"

"Yeah. Did you already eat?" He pokes his head into the family room to see his kids for the first time today. "Hello, girls."

Two voices echo from the dark room. "Hi, Daddy." The pair are lying on the sofa, entangled in a giant blanket. They're entranced by whatever's playing on the TV and don't bother to look in his direction.

"Nice to see you too," he teases and walks back toward the kitchen.

"They're tired," says Dandelion. She nods in the direction of the glowing screen. "It's a good thing there's only three and a half weeks of school left. They need a break and can't wait to go home for the summer."

"I think we all do." Oak pulls out a barstool and takes a seat. "Shit. I meant to grab a beer."

"Sit. I'll get you one. Your dinner's heating in the microwave." She makes her way over to the drinks' fridge, selects a bottle of lager, and pries off the crown. "Did you have a bad day?"

"Not bad, just long." He hops out of his seat to stop the microwave from beeping and pulls out the plate of steaming food. "This looks good."

"It's your favorite – chicken and dumplings. I used your mother's recipe." She grabs him a fork and places his foaming beer on the counter. "You look like you need this."

Oak takes a bite of the creamy chicken and says, "So, you know we need to find a place to live, right?"

"Duh." Dandie can't help herself from being snarky. It was a dumb question.

"Okay. Well, we have to go there."

"Uh-huh."

"Soon."

She isn't facing her husband because she's rinsing dinner plates and placing them into the dishwasher. "Oak, I'm very aware of what we need to do. Tell me, when would be a good time to drop everything and jet to Switzerland?" Her tone is flat and her lips are pursed. She reminds herself to rein in her bitchiness before turning around to face him. She can hear the girls giggling in the other room.

"I have no idea." Oak's chewing his food. "Do you have any thoughts about it? We're really late to the party." He's focused on his food and not looking at her.

"Oh," says Dandie, "I'm totally aware of how late to the party we are." In expat terms, they are months behind the process. They should've been looking at houses and schools in Zug at least three months ago. Dandelion stops doing the dishes and thinks about his question. *How can we do this? Think outside of the box.* There's not enough time to take the trip together before going back to the US for the summer. It's stupid to travel all the way to the US then travel back to Europe. *The jetlag will be a killer.* The girls will be bored out of their minds on a house-hunting trip and most likely annoying. Oak could kill two birds with one stone by going alone – a business trip and house hunt all in one. *Um. Hello!? No. I don't trust him to pick out a house by himself.* Or she could go alone. *Bingo.*

She picks up a dirty dish and rinses it before placing it in the dishwasher and then turns around and says with confidence, "I actually do have an idea." She doesn't want to appear too cocky because her idea might scare him. She's already picturing herself eating dinner al fresco at a lakeside bistro by herself.

"Lay it on me." Oak gets up from his dinner, walks over to the cabinet to grab a glass, and then fills it at the tap.

"What if I go alone?" She's standing with a straight back and has a determined look on her face.

"Really?" His head cocks to the side. He's looking confused. "When?"

"The same day we've already planned to travel back to the US. You and the girls can fly home per the original plan, and I can go to Switzerland to find a house and visit the school. When I'm done, I'll fly home." *I'm a fucking genius.*

"Don't you want me to be there with you?"

"Of course, but isn't this an easier way to handle it? I'm sure you know I'm capable of doing this on my own. I mean, let's be honest, Oak, it's not as if your opinion is really going to matter when it comes to choosing a house." Dandelion wipes crumbs from the counter. *C'mon, you know this is a brilliant idea.* "Besides, we have a loaded schedule from now until we leave for the US, and the calendar is chock full of visitors and plans back home already. This will create the least number of ripples." *And give me some well-deserved alone time.* "We'll be able to enjoy our summer holidays before coming back here to pack up the house and head to Zug."

"You want me to fly home with them all by myself?" he whispers. He motions his head in the direction of the next room.

"Well, it's not like I'm asking you to do something I haven't done for the past 10 years." Dandie's got enough ammo in her artillery to take this discussion nuclear. "If I recall, the first time I traveled alone internationally was from D.C. to Geneva with a two-year-old Thistle when I was seven months pregnant." *What else you got, dear?*

"But this is a long flight." It sounds as if he knows he's nearing defeat, but he gives one final push. "Twenty-seven hours door to door."

"You'll be sitting in business class, right? The flight attendants will take care of everything, which will be an upgrade from some of my past experiences. You won't have to nurse a baby, change diapers, or chase after a toddler in coach like I did when they were little." *Checkmate.* This is a chance for Oak to get a taste of what it's like to be Dandie.

"Okay. I'll ask the travel department to change your flights." He sits at the counter finishing his dinner in defeat. "Oh, I have to tell you something about our visas for Switzerland. You might want to sit down for this." Oak may have lost the battle, but he still has one bomb left to drop.

"What now?" She takes a seat next to him. *This can't be good.*

"I spoke to the immigration lawyers today and they said you need to pass a German language exam in order for my work visa to be renewed next year." He ducks his head to the side to cover his face from a potential punch.

"You're kidding, right?" She just can't even go there. "Do *you* have to take a test?"

"I'm not kidding," he says solemnly, "and no, I don't. Only you do."

"Just stop talking." It's bad enough she has to learn a new language in her 40s; now she's got his job riding on her less than stellar linguistic abilities. "I swear to god, Oak. You either married the right woman or a dumb one because I don't' know many who'd put up with this sort of garbage." Dandie might not always be prepared for the snafus of expat life, but she isn't going to let it get her down.

Be the woman you want your daughter to be

The girls' last day of school is full of tear-stained faces, walks down memory lane, laughter, and hugs that are hard to end. Thistle and Wivi are veterans of these scenarios. Every year of their short lives they've said goodbye to friends and familiar faces. Some years they're the ones leaving, but other times they're the ones being left behind. So they understand both sides of the goodbye.

Their mother sometimes forgets how resilient her daughters are when it comes to coping with change. These sass-filled sisters are just as brave as anyone. Their little worlds are like snow globes. Except these snow globes are charmed: when the snow finally settles on the bottom of its dome, an unfamiliar scene emerges.

The final bell of the school year rings, and a swarm of young, smiling faces scurries out of the school corridors. Some make their way to the line of school buses that are ready to depart for their final route of the year, while others crowd around the pick-up zone in small groups. When the buses depart, the crowd of parents and excited kids begins to thin.

The three of them climb into Dandelion's small white SUV, and Thistle and Wivi buckle up as their mom reverses from the parking spot. As they approach the exit of the school, they see crowds of familiar faces lining the street. The entire school staff is outside sending off the parade of buses and cars filled with students by waving, cheering, and shouting their last goodbyes. Dandelion can no longer hold it in and she starts to cry.

Wivi sees her mother trying to conceal her tears and asks, "You okay, Mom?"

"Yep. All good, honey."

"It's okay to cry," says Thistle. "I cried a lot today. Crying doesn't always have to be about sadness; it can be about good stuff too."

"She's right, Mom," Wivi pipes up.

This takes Dandelion by surprise. Wivi never thinks her older sister is right about *anything*.

"You know what my teacher told me today when I was crying at school? He said, Wivi, don't forget the Dr. Seuss quote we read the other day. 'Don't cry because it's over, smile because it happened.'"

We don't meet people by accident

How is this real life? thinks Dandie as she takes a seat at a breakfast table set for three and pours herself a glass of orange juice. The veranda of the safari lodge overlooks a watering hole with warthogs drinking at the edge, and in the distance, she can see a tower of giraffe grazing on the tops of acacia trees. *This view never gets old.*

She and her friends have been up for hours and already had a successful morning in the South African high veld watching a leopard pull a zebra into a tree while hyena circled below. *I'm glad I didn't sleep in*, thinks Dandelion, banging the dust off her pant legs as her friends take their seats at the table.

A waiter approaches with a tray of mimosas and sets one down in front of each of the women. "Your breakfast will be out in a moment. I do hope you had a good bush drive this morning." He turns and heads back to the kitchen without another word.

"I'm whooped, but that was amazing," declares Mags as she melts into her chair. "Put a fork in me, I'm done." Looking at Dandelion, she says, "I don't know how you are going to manage traveling tonight."

"Seriously," says Dahlia, "I'm exhausted. I love the morning bush rides, but man am I tired." She's keeping it together really well, but she knows this is going to be the last time these friends will be with her in South Africa.

The waiter returns. "Ladies, if I may…." He serves each of them a beautifully stacked eggs Benedict with perfectly poached eggs. "Bon appétit." He's gone before they can respond.

Dandelion picks up her fork and stabs the tangerine yolk, and it drips down the sides like streaks on a paint can. "Mags, what's your plan?"

"We're going to stick around here for another few days before schlepping back to the US for three weeks. We'll be bouncing between my mother's house and Chestnut's parents' condo. It's going to be miserable. It's bad enough I'll be living out of a suitcase for the foreseeable future; now I get to spend my holidays on a basement pullout sofa." She shakes her head. "And they say expat life is glamorous." The trio sniggers in agreement.

"Well, that's *no bueno*," says Dahlia shaking pepper onto her breakfast. "And you?" She's looking at Dandelion.

"We leave tonight. The girls and Oak leave around ten and I leave at midnight. But I'll be back in eight weeks to pack up the house, so you aren't rid of me quite yet." She smiles at Dahlia.

"I'm so excited for you," says Mags. "You're finally going to see where you're moving." Mags seems more eager than Dandie. "Actually, I'm just jealous. Sitting in business class by yourself and going out to eat every night without anyone complaining. It sounds like a fucking vacation." She laughs.

"Believe me, I'll be taking full advantage of the next five days even though it will be busy – because I totally deserve it." Dandelion lifts her glass. "To solo travel!"

Three glasses meet with a clink. "To solo travel!"

They pose for one final group shot in front of the high veld landscape before starting their journey back home. The two-hour car ride is a somber one, the result of early wake-up calls and too many bottles of wine at dinner.

The silence is broken by the dinging of Dahlia's phone. She reads the text and relays the message. "Spruce says to go to the clubhouse." She texts him back to say they're 20 minutes out.

As the three women approach, they see their husbands' cars lined up in the parking lot.

"Looks like they're having their own going away party," says Mags, smirking.

When they enter the dining area, the women are greeted by their families for one final Sunday lunch. "You didn't think we'd let this day go to waste, did you?" hollers Spruce from across the dining room.

The ladies make their way to the adult table and take a seat. They're each handed a glass flute by Spruce. He shoots a knowing look at Dahlia, and she nods in agreement. There are two empty seats where Rosey and Elm should be sitting.

"Dahlia and I gathered you all here one last time because, well, you jerks" – he motions to everyone except his wife – "are leaving us for new adventures. And even though we're sad to see you go, we're grateful to have been part of your stories. Not to mention we need to thank you for forcing us to meet some new people." He is simultaneously laughing and choked up. "Not to worry, we'll be using all of your homes as vacation spots over the next few years. At least you're moving to places we want to visit." He pauses. "To friendship; may it never know distance."

Remember when you wanted what you currently have?

O.R. Tambo International airport is empty when Dandelion arrives for her flight to Zurich. It's approaching 10 p.m. and most of the flights have already taken off for the evening. The solo traveler quickly checks in and gets her boarding pass. *Seat 2A; nice.* She makes her way through security with ease and then heads to the airport lounge where she's one of only two patrons. She selects a spot to sit and grabs herself a glass of shiraz and some food to nibble on while she waits for her flight to be called.

It feels luxurious to be traveling alone. Not having to herd children like cats through the corridors of the airport or constantly remind them not to forget their backpacks is bliss. Dandelion's only luggage is a small carry-on suitcase and a tote bag – easily managed with her two free hands because no one's asking her to carry their crap. Since she's traveling light to Switzerland, Oak took the rest of her summer items back with him and the girls. *Even though it's **#notmyproblem**, I wonder how Oak is doing at 30,000 feet.*

Swirling the burgundy velvet in her glass, Dandelion recalls the last time she traveled alone. Singapore. It's been just over a year since she felt the foundation of her character begin to quiver. She remembers sitting on the tarmac with tears spilling from her eyes and an ache in her heart for the woman she thought she'd lost. *Damn, have I come a long way.*

No longer is Dandelion just weathering the storm, she is confident, composed, and capable. *Even if some people think control of your own life is selfish. Oleander, PTA Petunia, and the Chatty Cactuses can **#kissmyass**.* She's also thrown overboard the distorted images of a person she believes others want or need her to be. She's proud of having the courage to unwrap a decade's worth of emotions and having the determination to tackle each one of them head-on.

She is tenacious. She is resilient. She is spirited, daring, genuine, and worthy. She is fucking brave. She is a ***#badass***.

An hour later she checks the flight information display to see her plane is ready to board. She collects her things, takes her last sip of wine, and makes her way to the gate. Stepping onto the gangway, Dandelion is nothing but ready to begin this new chapter of her life.

Yesterday I really wanted tacos. Now I'm eating tacos. Follow your dreams.

"I've been looking forward to talking to you – I can't believe we're having our final session together," says Sunflower enthusiastically. "I know you've had a lot going on lately. Where in the world are you right now?"

"I'm in Switzerland. I head to the US tomorrow." Dandelion's sitting in the window seat of her small but adequate hotel room. It looks out onto the old town square, where people are stopping traffic like magic as they approach the crosswalks and the Zugersee glistens in the distance between old buildings. It's nothing like Johannesburg.

Sunflower's face lights up at the word Switzerland. "Oh, right! How is it?"

"You know, it's been really good. I found a house and the school seems like a nice fit for my girls. While I was getting a school tour, the admissions director introduced me to a fellow American named PTA Pansy. She wasted no time telling me how volunteering was a great way to get involved in the community. I only met her for a moment, but I knew her motives. I kept thinking, *This isn't my first rodeo*." Lotus gives Dandelion the warm and fuzzies. "It's stunning here, just different from what we've gotten used to over the past few years. I forgot how expensive everything is and that they charge you for tap water." She rolls her eyes in annoyance.

"Yeah. It's not exactly a cheap place to live. I'm glad to hear you're having a productive trip, though." Sunflower's always a glass-half-full kind of woman. "So, what've you got planned for your summer?"

Dandelion leans back against the windowsill. "I'm putting my brain on cruise control."

"What do you mean by cruise control?" Sunflower is digging.

"I'm not going to overthink things too much. I'm tired of always tapping the brakes because I'm not sure if what I'm doing is correct. My mind is tired, and I don't have to think so hard at home in the US – I'm going to enjoy it because once we land in Switzerland, it'll be game on. This summer is a self-care vacation for my brain."

Dandelion loves her trips back to the US because her entire being goes on expat life hiatus. She's completely capable of doing all the stuff that needs to be done while living abroad, it just takes her a little longer compared to doing the exact same thing at home.

"Haha. I know what you mean about the overthinking part. It'll feel great to turn your brain off from worrying about moving for a while too."

Dandelion nods in agreement. "I mean, I'm sure I'll still think about it, but I won't be able to take action. What's done is done for now – plus, the house in Joburg is basically ready to be packed up. I took the advice from you and Mags and kyboshed the pity party I was having for myself and got my expat life in order."

Not having to micromanage the moving process for the next seven weeks is an unexpected gift from a less than ideal situation. There's no doubt she wishes she could rewrite this excerpt of her life, but it's just not possible.

"If this move was happening a year ago, I would've been a total mess. But I'm in such a different place now. I'm so proud of myself. And you know me, I don't like to blow smoke up my own ass, but it's true. It feels really good just being me."

Dandelion catches a glimpse of herself in the reflection of the window and admires what she sees – her casual self in jeans and t-shirt. Her hair is a ball of curls and there's barely any makeup on her sun-kissed face. It's been a long time coming, but she's comfortable in her own skin again. Dandie is like a snake shedding its skin to allow for continued growth and ridding itself of the parasites that cling to it. The past doesn't determine her future.

Sunflower stands up and starts clapping. It's a very small standing ovation. "Congratulations, Dandelion. It's not often someone can say that about themselves. You have officially achieved BadASSery."

"Thank you," replies Dandelion, getting up from her chair and taking a bow. "A year ago, I would've swept your compliments aside. But look at me now. I guess that's what becoming a badass does to you."

#MYTHEORY

C.S. Lewis wrote: "You can't go back and change the beginning, but you can start where you are and change the ending." I love this quote because it gives the reader permission to modify their life without dwelling on the past. I think this idea is an enormous act of self-love. For the rest of my life, I'll be a student of this logic because each passing day teaches me something new. Going forward, I'm positive I won't be happy with some of my life experiences, but hey, I can't change what's done – so I need to keep moving forward. Harping on about 'what ifs' and 'should haves' isn't going to get me anywhere. There's no time like the present to get our asses in gear and start following the needle on the compass.

I like who I'm becoming

For years, I dreamed of feeling completely comfortable in my own skin. No, I'm not talking about my dress size. I'm talking about the whole package – mind, body, and soul. Upon reflection, it's the real reason I went through the coaching process. I initially thought it was to find my purpose (insert eye roll), but it gave me so much more than that.

Along the way, I figured out a couple of very important things. First, my idea of purpose didn't involve finding, manifesting, or creating a career. I'm not ruling out a career of some sort in the future because there are lots of things I want to be when I grow up, but a job definitely wasn't what I needed at that point in my life. I already had enough jobs that didn't pay or allow for vacation days. So why would I want to add more stress? What I really wanted was to enjoy the life I was already living.

And second, I wasn't interested in allowing someone else's ideas define me. I'd gotten so sick and tired of hearing boss babes spew their 'hustle harder' bullshit. Pushing me to keep up with all the other hot messes out there wasn't going to motivate me. Coincidentally, those women are probably just trying to get through the fucking day too, and skewing our views of what we should be doing isn't going to make us better – it's going to make us feel less and less confident. I'm all for empowering women, but I sure as hell don't need any more added pressure to perform from outside influences. Believe me, I've already got enough voices in my head.

You were my cup of tea, but I drink champagne now

The coaching process helped me figure out how to be whole again. None of it was rocket science, but it did involve shifting my mindset. The collective nature of the work I did was reinforced by each piece of key learning. I wouldn't have been able to regain my confidence, rebuild my self-identity, or restructure how I lived my life if I hadn't implemented all sorts of key changes that were complementary to one another.

1. **I shushed my inner critic**
    With my inner mean girl no longer in control and my gut in check, it was easier for me to overcome the daily challenges that expat life dished out. With each of these little wins, my confidence grew. I no longer found myself holding back from putting myself into circumstances that would've previously made me uncomfortable – because I trusted myself to make the right decision. My boosted

confidence also helped me tackle other insecurities and see the humor in life. I became less self-conscious and more outspoken.

2. **I quit allowing others to tell me who I was**
   My identity crisis went buh-bye when I took the time to reexamine who I was in the present — my passions, my vision, and my values. I'd changed an enormous amount during those first ten years abroad, and I was no longer aligned with the person I used to be. The new me and the old me were the same person, just different. I also stopped placing value on the approval or opinion of others, which made me see the worth of my own views so much more. Being able to think for yourself is so empowering.

3. **I altered my view of purpose**
   Remember the *something* that'd been missing? Well, it got filled with a whole lot of things I'd thought were insignificant aspects of my life. I became more satisfied with intentional living. Writing for the sake of it rewards the creative part of my mind, nurturing meaningful relationships benefits my soul, and taking time each day to focus on my health strengthens my body. Of course, there's the mundane life stuff like dirty dishes in the sink and picking up dog poop in the yard, but the deliberate choices I make create happiness and fulfillment within me.

As I closed in on the end of my coaching process, I really noticed significant changes in how I lived my life. I no longer felt like the 'wife of.' Instead, I embodied the clever, accomplished, and fierce badass I'd always been — I just finally owned it. I'm so proud of my decision to take a chance on me and my happiness. I didn't realize what kind of influence the process would have on my life. To give you a visual, imagine every nuance of change as a single-stemmed flower. If I draw together all these stems of change (and there are a lot), the final product would be a bouquet of bold transformation. Individually the flowers are beautiful, but together they make a striking statement.

You are magic. Own that shit.

I didn't wake up one morning and tell myself, "Claire, today you'll be a badass." Instead, it took time, patience, and a lot of fucking work. I've emphasized the absolute requirement of hard work because I believe in a healthy work ethic. It means you have grit and won't stop until the job is done. If something is important to you, you'll work like hell to make it happen. This isn't the kind of work you can pawn off on someone else to do. This is all on you.

So, I challenge you to show up for yourself. Not because you're a trailing spouse, but because you're fucking worthy of badassery. It's there for the taking; it's up to you to make it happen.

Epilogue

I always wanted to write a book but had no idea what I'd ever write about. Nor did I think it would end up being so personal. Some topics in this book were extremely difficult to write. In many ways, reflecting on a time in my life that was polarizing made me long for the good stuff, like my friends, so much more. You see, I began writing this book during a time when I was grieving my South African life and transitioning to the new Swiss one. These pages were written with the peaks of the Swiss Alps in the distance – a dramatic backdrop to the latest episode of *My Crazy Expat Life: In der Schweiz version 2.0.*

Completing the writing process took a lot longer than I expected: over two years. Which is probably way too long for some and not long enough for others. But remember, we all bloom in our own time, and I'm so happy for those who manage to do things better than me. I will admit, though, it wasn't from lack of trying. The Covid-19 pandemic hit six months after we moved to Switzerland, and it shuttered the world. You'd think not being able to go anywhere or see anyone would accelerate my creative process. On the contrary. I'm the kind of person who works well when it's quiet, not when I can hear my kids screaming at each other from too much togetherness or complaining that the Wi-Fi is too slow.

I also wrote this book in my spare time – you know, when I wasn't playing taxi driver, private chef, dog walker, cleaner, personal shopper, bookkeeper, health advocate, loving mother, and wife. Moonlighting is no joke, and I give a shit ton of kudos to anyone who does it. I found it hard to carve out time to concentrate during the day because so much of my life was pulling me in other directions, and I felt guilty for not doing what needed to be done. Yes, I know what you're going to say: "But Claire, why didn't you implement boundaries or time for yourself?" Believe me, I tried, but the creative process doesn't always work Monday through Friday from 2–4 p.m.

Instead, there were many late nights staring into the brightly-lit screen of my laptop when I should've been in bed. I burned the midnight oil because I was in the flow, and I did everything I could to seize those moments. I felt no FOMO with this kind of sacrifice because there was a really good chance I wasn't going to be able to sleep anyway. Let's be realistic: someone was going to be snoring in bed next to me, or my brain was going to keep me awake worrying about what I should cook for dinner the next day, or a dog was going to barf. This kind of sacrifice didn't make me feel like I was losing out, because it fueled my mind, body, and soul. So I embraced it – and the dark circles under my eyes.

I won't quit, but I will cuss the whole time

Speaking of embracing things, I want to say something about all the tidbits of advice I offered you in this book. I'm sure, at times, reading the *#MyTheory* sections felt like drinking from a fire hose. Sorry about that, but I couldn't stop myself from giving you as much ammo as I could to help you embody the badass you already are. I've honestly done all the things I wrote about, but not all at the same time. If you did attempt this, you'd probably go a little bonkers. Some things can be more effective than others, and what can be really successful in the beginning can wear off later on. So you might need to change things up on occasion. We are different animals, and you've gotta find what works for you.

Every single day I work on this stuff. And every single day I falter. I will never claim to be a master of my own domain. I have more control over it, but I'm not perfect and never will be. I still have moments of madness, but now I have a better handle on how to make them shorter and less frequent. On occasion, I get overwhelmed, let my inner critic control my mind, and feel lonely in a crowd of people. I continually practice being the most authentic version of me, but it's not always easy. So when I'm riding the struggle bus toward Shitsville, I make sure I give myself the gifts of grace, patience, and a hell of a lot of love.

I may not be there yet, but I'm closer than I was yesterday

As this book was nearing completion, I began searching for my next project to dive into. I don't do well with idle hands and I was ready for another challenge and another tattoo. I had no idea what the challenge was going to be, but the tattoo will be, you guessed it, a dandelion blowing in the wind. After a little more digging with my personal coach, I figured out what the challenge would be. Now, before I tell you what I decided to do, I'm already cringing because it sounds a bit cliché. But in my heart of hearts, I feel good about my choice because I followed my heart and my intuition, not my fearmongering inner critic – and that little demon had her claws out trying to talk me out of this decision.

I chose to become a coach and mentor for expat women. Not as a job – a 9 to 5 – but because I wanted to do something fulfilling. It wasn't a decision I made lightly, but I figure if I can help at least one woman from feeling like a flailing spouse, it'll be totally worth all the time and effort. I'm enjoying the process of learning again, and the idea of adding a new skill to my personal arsenal of knowledge feels pretty badass to me.

I still continue to write my blog, *My Theory On Blooming*, where I theorize about whatever random thing pops into my head. I've been writing it for over 10 years now, and it's amazing how my writing skills have improved in that period. Imagine what I might be capable of in another 10 years.

If you'd like to learn more about me, check out my blog, or inquire about coaching services, you can go to www.clairehauxwell.com for more information. You can also follow me on Instagram at @mytheoryonblooming.

Acknowledgments

Writing a book is one of the hardest things I've ever done. Each day I'd sit in front of my laptop questioning my decision to tell my story. Was I writing something that needed to be read by others? Did I have the stamina to complete such a project? Was I going to make a fool of myself? The answers to those questions are yes, yes, and who the hell cares. I'm so grateful I didn't listen to that voice in my head.

This book wouldn't exist if I hadn't had an incredible support system of friends and family cheering me on for the past two years. Yes, I know, it probably shouldn't have taken me two years to write, but I'd never lived through a global pandemic before and didn't realize every shred of sanity I had would be used to cook homemade meals all day long and to endure a soundtrack of bickering and barking that was stuck on repeat. I'll try harder next time. But to everyone who had a hand in being a village helper during this process, I can't thank you enough. You're good people.

I'm so thankful for my writing mentor, Jo Parfitt. She believed in my literary idea and guided me through the process of making this book a reality. She responded to my initial proposal with, "Yes, I love your idea, and if your voice is strong and sassy and witty and no-crap Hauxwell, then you have a good idea that's time has come." I wasn't ready for her response but thought it sounded like a challenge that needed to be accepted.

The current version of me wouldn't exist, let alone be able to write a book, if I hadn't found my coach, Sundae Bean. She helped me out of a dark place and walked beside me as I rose above my mountain of limiting bullshit. Working with her changed my life so much that I decided to become a coach myself. There is no better feeling than truly being seen, ugly cry and all, by someone who believes in you. And for that, I thank her.

A big shout-out to my daughters, Elyse and Addilyn. I know your mother "working" still seems like a novel idea to you both, but I'm glad you decided to run with it. Neither of you ever go hungry, you're always picked up from school, and you never run out of clean clothes to wear. Know that these are my weird ways of saying I love you and that being your mom is the best job I'll ever have.

I owe a load of gratitude to my husband, Dave. He's always there to make me laugh and keep me on my toes. Yes, I'm sure he thinks I'm totally nuts at times, but overall, he has an awesome wife trying to keep up with him and his antics. And by antics, I mean moving me around the world. I love you and our unconventional life, and I couldn't imagine living it with anyone else.

A special thanks to my very first role model, my mom. Growing up, she taught me so many things – how to cook a perfect pot roast, how to sew the ribbons on my pointe shoes, and the proper way to clean a toilet. She also taught me resilience, tenacity, and the value of hard work. I suppose I owe her a lot more for dealing with the independent fireball I was during my teen years. I love you, Mom, and thanks for being exactly who I needed you to be.

About the author

Claire Hauxwell is a professional badass, writer, author, and coach. A trained supply chain professional and ex-spreadsheet lover, she now puts her Type A personality to work by deconstructing the nuances of expat life. With more than a decade of global living experience, Claire shares her wisdom on her *My Theory On Blooming* blog and coaches female expat accompanying spouses to create fulfilling and intentional lives abroad. If she's not roaming the aisles of the grocery store or meandering the forest with her dogs, you'll find her sweating it out at CrossFit or having cocktails with friends. Claire and her family currently live in Switzerland but every summer return to the shores of Muskegon, Michigan, for a taste of home.

www.clairehauxwell.com
claire@clairehauxwell.com

Designed by

www.ingramcontent.com/pod-product-compliance
Lightning Source LLC
Chambersburg PA
CBHW071729080526
44588CB00013B/1951